The Legacy
of Wittgenstein

The Legacy
of Wittgenstein

ANTHONY   KENNY

Basil Blackwell

© Anthony Kenny 1984

First published 1984

Basil Blackwell Publisher Ltd
108 Cowley Road, Oxford OX4 1JF, UK

Basil Blackwell Inc.
432 Park Avenue South, Suite 1505,
New York, NY 10016, USA

British Library Cataloguing in Publication Data
Kenny, Anthony
The legacy of Wittgenstein.
1. Wittgenstein, Ludwig
I. Title
192   B3376.W564

ISBN 0–631–13705–X

Typeset by Katerprint Co Ltd, Oxford
Printed in Great Britain at Camelot Press Ltd, Southampton

Contents

Introduction

Some ten years ago I published an elementary introduction to the philosophy of Wittgenstein. I believed, as did many others in the Anglo-American philosophical world, that Wittgenstein was the most significant philosopher of the present century and that his contributions to philosophy of language and of mind constituted an irreversible advance in the subject. I expected that as his insights were absorbed, particularly by younger thinkers, their influence would be felt widely not only among philosophers but by scientists working in many disciplines. I hoped that my book would help to introduce the general public to ideas with which they would increasingly want to be familiar.

The experience of the last decade has been chastening for those who think that Wittgenstein's work is important and should be more widely appreciated. The philosopher's influence seems to be declining rather than increasing. It is true that Wittgenstein's writings are now much more widely read in France and Germany and other countries outside the Anglo-American tradition. It is true that within that tradition itself we have seen the incessant publication of further posthumous works from the *Nachlass*, and the appearance of scholarly commentaries on the great *Philosophical Investigations*. Indeed, we might say that Wittgensteinian scholarship has blossomed during the decade, though there is still no definitive edition of his main works nor even any agreement about what form such an edition might take. But Wittgensteinian philosophy, as opposed to Wittgensteinian scholarship, has not made progress and some of the philosophical gains we owe to Wittgenstein seem in danger of being lost. This is not because his work has been superseded or put in the shade by the light of some succeeding philosophical genius. Rather, his contribution has been neglected because more and more philosophers, especially in the United States, have attempted to model their studies on the pattern of a rigorously scientific discipline, mimicking the type of precision characteristic of mathematics, and holding up a general theory of linguistics as the ideal for philosophy of language, and an abstract system for artificial intelligence as the goal of philosophy of mind. This kind of scientism in philosophy was something which Wittgenstein abominated, and in such a climate the seeds he planted have a poor chance of flourishing growth.

I continue to believe that there are many areas of philosophy, and many fields of scientific endeavour, in which really fruitful work is unlikely to be done by anyone who has not absorbed what Wittgenstein has to teach. Those who ignore Wittgenstein's critique of false philosophy and pseudo-science take the risk of constructing imposing edifices of thought which turn out to be nothing but houses of cards. One can say this without necessarily accepting the view, suggested by some passages in Wittgenstein, and endorsed by some Wittgensteinians, that the task of philosophy is wholly negative and destructive: while the destruction of intellectual garbage is a wholesome and necessary function, it need not be the only function of the philosopher.

In my introductory book *Wittgenstein* I emphasized the continuity of the philosopher's thought: it was a mistake to regard the philosophy of the *Philosophical Investigations* as quite divorced from that of the early *Tractatus Logico-Philosophicus*. 'How can people say there are two Wittgensteins?' I once asked a well-known Wittgensteinian, 'Now that the works of his middle period have been published you have to choose between one Wittgenstein and three.' 'No', he said, 'the choice is between one and four: you have forgotten *On Certainty*.'

Like my earlier book, this collection of essays is devoted to stressing the continuity of Wittgenstein's philosophy and of his conception of the nature of philosophy, and to illustrating the relevance of his work to the study of language and mind whether by the philosopher or the scientist. It aims to contribute both to Wittgensteinian scholarship and Wittgensteinian philosophy.

Of the ten essays in this book the first four are devoted to the study of Wittgenstein's own ideas, while the remaining six endeavour to apply these ideas to the works of other thinkers and the problems discussed by other philosophers. All are concerned with the three major themes of Wittgenstein's work: the nature of philosophy, the nature of language, and the nature of mind. Together they illustrate the wide ramifications of Wittgenstein's thought not only in the field of philosophy, but also in the area of empirical disciplines such as psychology, linguistics and the life sciences.

Anyone who compares Wittgenstein's *Tractatus* with his later writing is bound to be struck by the enormous difference between the proportion of the latter which is taken up with philosophy of mind, and the few cryptic remarks devoted to the topic in the former. Many of the issues which Wittgenstein came to regard as central to philosophy were assigned, in his early work, to empirical psychology as irrelevant to the real task of the philosopher. The first essay in this collection pieces together, from the brief passages in *Tractatus*, 3–3.5 and 5.541–5.5423, Wittgenstein's early philosophy of mind: the nature of thought, its relationship to propositions and propositional signs, and the analysis of propositions reporting belief and judgment. I argue that for the *Tractatus* reports of mental states are pseudo-propositions: they attempt to combine a factual report of a certain psychological state with an expression of the unsayable reality that the psychic elements of that state have the meaning they do, a meaning which must be conferred on them by the metaphysical self which is beyond the purview of psychology.

While the philosophy of mind of the *Tractatus* is profoundly unsatisfactory, and poles apart from that of the *Philosophical Investigations*, none the less the two works have in common two theses of fundamental importance: first, that introspectionist psychology can never explain meaning; and secondly that the ultimate creation of meaning is indescribable. As he developed away from the stance of the *Tractatus*, I argue in the second essay, Wittgenstein tended systematically to exaggerate the inadequacies of his earlier work in a way which masks the underlying continuity of his thought even in the areas where his changes of mind were most dramatic. I try to show that he came to misrepresent the *Tractatus* on the nature of names, on the nature of objects, on the nature of facts, and on the nature of propositions, with the effect that he overestimated the distance which separated the picture theory of meaning from that of the *Philosophical Investigations*. What is attacked in Wittgenstein's later work, I maintain, is sometimes not the real *Tractatus* but a mere ghost of it. Not that Wittgenstein did not have some of the thoughts which he later repudiated with scorn; but they belong rather to the period of his return to philosophy in the late twenties.

The intermediate period between the return and the writing of the *Philosophical Investigations* is the subject of the third essay. The most impressive product of the philosopher's work in the early thirties is a text nicknamed the 'Big Typescript' which probably dates from 1933. It was clearly conceived as a stage in a work for publication, though not at all a final one; some of it, after extensive revision, survived into the posthumously published *Investigations.*, The Big Typescript itself has never been published in its entirety; an edition of it, with drastic revision and pruning guided by Wittgenstein's own later thoughts, was published by Rush Rhees in 1969. I made an English version of this edition, which was published in 1974; in the course of working on that translation, I came to appreciate how many layers of editorial work, some by Wittgenstein and some by Rhees, lay between the Big Typescript and the published *Philosophical Grammar*. The third essay of this book is intended to give the reader a fuller account of this editorial intervention than is offered in Rhees' own modest editorial note to the German text. Apart from providing useful background information for readers of the *Philosophical Grammar*, the essay illustrates the problems which lie in wait for anyone who may eventually attempt to produce a definitive scholarly edition of Wittgenstein's *Nachlass*.

My third essay ends with the hope that Wittgenstein's executors will some day offer to the public the substantial portions of the Big Typescript which are inadequately represented in the published *Philosophical Grammar*. The fourth essay gives an indication of the interesting nature of one of these omitted passages, the section on the nature of philosophy. In that essay I discuss Wittgenstein's view of philosophy during the central period of his life, starting from the problem that he seems to present two different views of the discipline: philosophy as therapy for the sick understanding, and philosophy as an overview of language and of the world. I emphasize his hostility to the view that philosophy deals with the foundations of knowledge, providing, in Descartes' metaphor, the roots of the tree of science. This is what lies behind Wittgenstein's well-known remark that the real discovery is the one that makes him capable of stopping doing philosophy when he wants to.

'Why do philosophy', Wittgenstein asked himself, 'if it is only useful against philosophers?' The reason, I suggest, is that there is a philosopher in each of us, against whom we need to be on our guard: we must, if the occasion arises, exorcise the bad implicit philosophy which we imbibe unknowingly as we acquire language; philosophy will enable us to avoid this bewitchment to which we are subject as to an original sin. The essay ends by asking the question whether there can be progress in philosophy: is it a cumulative science, or is it a discipline which each person must administer to himself afresh?

This final question of the first part of the book leads on to the second part which begins with three essays which relate Wittgenstein's work to three philosophers of three different periods: Aquinas, Descartes and Russell. In the eyes of many people, Wittgenstein's importance in the history of philosophy, and in particular of the philosophy of mind, lies especially in his criticism of the Cartesian framework within which philosophy and psychology had been conducted throughout the modern era, well beyond the critique of Kant. One side effect of Wittgenstein's liberation of philosophy from Cartesian prejudices is that it enables those who accept it to give a more sympathetic welcome to the writings of pre-Cartesian philosophers, and in particular to medieval scholastics. I argued for this in the earliest philosophical paper I published, 'Aquinas and Wittgenstein', in the *Downside Review* of 1960. That paper now seems to me too naive in detail to be taken very seriously, and I have not reproduced it here. But the fifth essay of the present collection, 'Intentionality', makes a comparison between the answers given by Aquinas and Wittgenstein to the question, 'What makes a thought of X be a thought *of X?*'

Aquinas' answer to this question is the theory of the immaterial intentional existence of forms in the mind. Wittgenstein's answer is a reminder of the language game that we play when we write a name underneath a portrait. At first sight the two answers seem to belong to different worlds. In this essay I try to show that the two answers are complementary, each concerned with a part of the problem of intentionality, Aquinas' with the sense of our thoughts and Wittgenstein's with their reference. If we combine the insights of the two philosophers, I argue, we can give an account of the nature of thought which enables us to avoid the realist idealism of the Platonists without falling into the conceptualist idealism of popular anti-realism. Aquinas' account of the nature of universals enables us to combine the objective Fregean view of a concept as the reference of a predicate with the subjective Wittgensteinian notion of a concept as the learnt mastery of a word.

The sixth paper in the collection deals directly with the conflict between the Wittgensteinian and the Cartesian approach to the philosophy of mind, at the point at which Descartes' myth has the most powerful hold on our imagination, namely the first person. The paper originally appeared as a tribute to Professor G.E.M. Anscombe, who first brought me to realize the importance of the liberating insights of Wittgenstein. I argue that the power of Cartesian ideas is so strong that it can exert a strong influence even on those most firmly seized of their ultimate untenability. I claim that even Professor Anscombe, in the account which she gives of our use of the first person, has not totally exorcised the spirit of the Cartesian ego. I do my best to supplement the account she gives of I-sentences in a manner which takes full account of Wittgenstein's critique of private languages.

The seventh paper, like the fifth, deals with the problem of intentionality and the analysis of reports of meaningful utterances and mental states. It was written as a reply to a paper by the late Arthur Prior in a symposium on *Oratio Obliqua*. It transpired that the main difference between the account Prior gave and the one I wished to give turned on the fact that Prior accepted in its essentials the account of proper names given by Bertrand Russell while I regarded that account as having been exploded by Wittgenstein in the *Philosophical Investigations*. Much of the paper is taken up, therefore, with an attempt to present a non-Russellian account of proper names, taking account of Wittgenstein's criticisms. The topics of the essay have been the subject of much discussion in recent years, due to the writings of Kripke and others. If I were writing on the topic now, I would write slightly differently to take account of some of the commonplaces of recent discussion; but the arguments of the paper are still relevant to, and in some places anticipate, the contemporary discussion. I have not tried to rewrite it in the fashionable idiom, but I have adapted it in detail to make it an independent essay, removing the explicit references to the preceding discussion of Prior.

In the last three papers of the collection I try to illustrate how thinkers other than philosophers can gain from assimilating the teaching of Wittgenstein. I discuss the work of three writers, each of them celebrated in different fields of scientific endeavour, and show how their writing displays traces of an uncritical acceptance of philosophical prejudices which had been decisively criticized by Wittgenstein. The three writers are Teilhard de Chardin, R.L. Gregory, and Noam Chomsky. The damaging effect of the unconscious Cartesianism varies greatly from one of these to the other: in the case of Gregory it does no more than mar the style of presentation with a risk of confusing the unwary reader; in the case of Teilhard de Chardin it vitiates the entire system.

The eighth essay in this collection was the first to be published: it was a review of Teilhard's major work. *The Phenomenon of Mind*, which appeared a few months before the book was magisterially demolished by Professor Peter Medawar in a memorable review in *Mind* (recently republished in *Pluto's Republic*). As Medawar's review showed, one did not have to be a Wittgensteinian to see that the work was fatally flawed; but in my review I concentrated on the fact that Teilhard's claim to be writing a purely scientific thesis could not bear scrutiny because he was basing himself on, and extrapolating from, a set of Cartesian assumptions about the nature of consciousness, assumptions which were the targets of Wittgenstein's decisive attack. Teilhard's philosophical misunderstanding of the nature of consciousness meant that his reflections on the relationship between consciousness and complexity in the course of evolution, and his projection of that course forward towards an Omega point of supreme consciousness and love, could not be taken seriously.

My review, published at a time when Teilhard was extremely fashionable in progressive Catholic circles, drew a number of hostile replies. In answer I developed the Wittgenstein argument against the Cartesian view of consciousness espoused by Teilhard. This answer, shorn of detailed references to the points made by critics of my review, appears as part II of the eighth chapter of this book.

The picture of consciousness which vitiates Teilhard's work is not, of course, peculiar to him. On the contrary, I have argued that it pervades the thought of scientists in several disciplines from the time of Descartes up to the present day. Its essence is the detachment of the concept of consciousness from its manifestation in activity and life. 'Only of a human being', wrote Wittgenstein, 'and what resembles (behaves like) a human being can one say: it has sensations; it sees; is blind; hears; is deaf; is conscious or unconscious.' In the ninth essay I illustrate the neglect of this dictum in areas such as psychology and artificial intelligence, where predicates whose normal application is to human beings are applied, without due precaution, to other entities such as brains or computers. I called the reckless application of human-being predicates to insufficiently human-like objects the 'homunculus fallacy', and this nickname gave its title to the essay. I gave examples of the occurrence of the fallacy in Descartes – who was in fact the first person to draw explicit attention to it – and in the work on perception of R.L. Gregory. The essay concludes with a postscript designed to prevent certain misunderstandings, which in its earlier version was a reply to a criticism of my paper by Professor Amélie Rorty.

In the tenth and final essay I turn from psychology to linguistics to illustrate the scientific relevance of Wittgenstein's philosophy. Noam Chomsky has argued that we may usefully think of the language faculty as a mental organ, analogous to the heart or the visual system; there is no clear demarcation line, he says, between physical organs, perceptual and motor systems, and cognitive faculties. In my essay I argue that Chomsky's view of mental structures involves a philosophical confusion. The confusion is sometimes nicknamed the 'hardware – software fallacy'; but this nickname is unfortunate since the postulated structures appear to be intended to be too ghostly to be hardware and too concrete to be software. I suggest that the root of Chomsky's confusion is his failure to distinguish between two different kinds of evidence which we may have for states of affairs: to distinguish between criteria and symptoms, in the terms introduced by Wittgenstein.

All the essays in this collection have appeared before, over a period of some twenty years. Though I have revised them to delete references to original contexts which are no longer relevant, I have not attempted to rewrite them to take account of the development of my thought during the period, and the reader will notice changes of mind on certain topics, though my overall view of the issues in the philosophy of mind, and of Wittgenstein's significance in that field, has not changed.

The first essay was published in *Perspectives on the Philosophy of Wittgenstein*, edited by Irving Block (Blackwell, 1981) and the second in *Understanding Wittgenstein*, edited by G.N.A. Vesey (Macmillan, 1974). Essay 3 was my contribution to the *Festschrift* for G.H. von Wright which was published in 1976 as volume 28 of *Acta Philosophica Fennica*. Essay 4, having appeared originally in German, was first published in English in *Wittgenstein and his Times*, edited by Brian McGuinness (Blackwell, 1982). The fifth essay is unpublished at the time of writing this introduction, but is forthcoming in a Pelican collection of essays on the history of philosophy, edited by Ted Honderich. Essay 6 first appeared in *Intention and Intentionality*, the Festschrift for G.E.M. Anscombe, edited by C. Diamond and J. Teichman (Harvester, 1979). Essay 7 was a reply to Arthur Prior's paper '*Oratio Obliqua*' in the Aristotelian Society symposium which was published in the society's Supplementary Proceedings for 1963. The review of Teilhard de Chardin's *The Phenomenon of Man* which appears as essay 8 was published in the *Bulletin of the Newman Association for the Philosophy of Mind* in 1960. Essay 9 was published in 1971 in *Interpretations of Life and Mind*, edited by Marjorie Grene (Routledge), and essay 10 appeared in the *Philosophical Transactions of the Royal Society* in 1981. I am most grateful to those concerned for granting the necessary permissions for the reproduction of these papers.

1

Wittgenstein's Early Philosophy
of Mind

'Theory of knowledge', said Wittgenstein in the *Tractatus* (4.1121),
'is the philosophy of psychology.' The context makes clear that
Erkenntnistheorie does not mean epistemology, if epistemology is an
inquiry into the justification of beliefs, the possibility of knowledge,
and the tenability or refutability of scepticism. Rather, it means
what is nowadays called 'philosophy of mind' – an analysis of
sentences reporting beliefs, judgments, perception and the like (cf.
5.541). Psychology is one of the natural sciences: the philosophy of
psychology will do for it what philosophy, according to the
Tractatus, is to do for each of the sciences; it will clarify its thought
and draw limits to its competence (4.112, 4.113).

Two sections of the *Tractatus* are devoted to this enterprise. The
passages in *Tractatus*, 3–3.5, linking Wittgenstein's general theory of
representation to his theory that a proposition is a picture, tell us
much about the nature of thoughts and thinking (*Gedanke* and
denken). *Tractatus*, 5.541–5.5423 discusses the analysis of such
propositions as 'A believes that *p*', 'A has the thought that *p*', 'A
judges that *p*', 'A perceives *p*', with the immediate purpose of
showing how these propositions are not exceptions to the rule that
propositions can occur in other propositions only as bases of truth
operations.

It has been the custom of commentators to discuss these passages
in comparative isolation from each other. It may even be questioned whether they do deal with the same topic at all. Is the
Gedanke of the 3s a psychological matter at all? May it not have
more in common with Frege's Platonic entity than with the topic of
Russell's theory of judgment? The clearest evidence that a *Gedanke*

is psychological comes in a letter from Wittgenstein to Russell in 1919. 'What are the constituents of a *Gedanke*?' Russell had asked. 'I don't know what the constituents of a thought are but I know *that* it must have such constituents which correspond to the words of Language. Again the kind of relation of the constituents of the thought and the pictured fact is irrelevant, it would be a matter of psychology to find out.' A *Gedanke* did not consist of words, but 'of psychical constituents that have the same sort of relation to reality as words'. This is unequivocal: but one might wish it did not follow an exegesis of the meaning of '*Sachverhalt*' and '*Tatsache*' which is notoriously difficult to reconcile with the actual text of the *Tractatus*. Direct evidence from the text of the 2s and 3s is not so explicit: still, a thought is a picture, and pictures are things which *we* make (3.2); thinking is something that *we* do (3.03); and a thought is something which unless expressed in a propositional sign is imperceptible by the senses (3.1). Clearly, then, it is neither a Platonic proposition nor a perceptible sentence: a psychological fact, the holding of a relation between psychic elements, as described by Wittgenstein to Russell, would certainly fit these requirements. I shall therefore assume that the thinking discussed in the 3s and early 4s is the same as the thinking discussed in 5.541ff.

The first thing that we are told about a thought is that it is a logical picture of facts; a logical picture, we have already been told, is a picture whose pictorial form is logical form (2.181), and pictorial form is what a picture must have in common with the reality it depicts (2.17). Pictures may have more than logical form in common with what they depict – a spatial picture, for instance, has spatial form in common with what it depicts – but every picture must have at least logical form in common (2.18). In this sense every picture is a logical picture: what then are we to make of the statement that a thought is a logical picture? There seem to be two ways in which we could take it: either as meaning that every picture is a thought, or as meaning that a thought was a picture whose pictorial form was *only* logical form. Against the former interpretation we must count the fact that thought seems to be related so closely to a proposition as to be capable of being identified with it (4); and whereas all propositions are pictures, there is no reason to think that the *Tractatus* regards all pictures as propositions. In favour of the latter is the fact that it is quite natural, and was long traditional, to regard the mental and the physical as distinct realms whose inhabitants had no properties in common: so that a psychic fact and the physical fact it depicted could have nothing in common beyond the bare logical form.[1]

The relation between thought and proposition is variously described by Wittgenstein: in 3.1 the proposition *expresses* the thought; in 4 the proposition is the thought. There is no contradiction here, only a verbal carelessness: like every great philosopher Wittgenstein was inconsistent in his use of his own technical terms. In 3.12 Wittgenstein introduced the term '*Satzzeichen*' ('propositional sign') for the perceptible state of affairs – the holding of a relation between written or spoken words or code-signs in more substantial hardware (3.1433) – which expresses the thought. So far as it expresses a thought, the propositional sign is a projection of a possible state of affairs (3.11–12). Just as a propositional sign can only be a proposition if projected by a thought on to the world, so a relationship holding between psychic elements can only be a thought if it is a projection, an application, of a propositional sign (3.5). This last sentence, in Wittgenstein's thought, is formally analogous to: Just as a man can only be a husband if married to a wife, so a woman can only be a wife if married to a man. The propositional sign, plus the thought, is the proposition; the thought is what gives the proposition its sense; a little loosely, we can say that thought *is* the sense-full proposition (*sinnvolle Satz*: proposition with its sense; not sensible as opposed to senseless proposition, for strictly speaking there is no such thing as a proposition without sense).

3.11, 3.12 and the 3.14s discuss various features of the *Satzzeichen* or propositional sign. 3.13 does not mention the propositional sign, but makes various remarks about the proposition (*Satz*). In the *Prototractatus* this passage occurred in a different, later, context. The fact that Wittgenstein moved it here suggests that he realized that what it contained illuminated the notion of *Satzzeichen* more than it illuminated that of *Satz*. He did not, however, make the changes in

---

[1] But would they not have temporality in common? And what of thoughts about thoughts? The first question is not answered either in the *Tractatus* or this paper: the second is answered at 5.541 and below.

vocabulary that would have rendered it totally appropriate to its new context. A reading of it, however, suggests that it makes much better sense if we distinguish within it between *Satz* and *Satzzeichen*. The passage – difficult to understand on any interpretation – runs as follows.

Zum Satz gehört alles, was zur Projektion gehört; aber nicht das Projizierte. Also die Möglichkeit des Projizierten, aber nicht dieses selbst.

A proposition includes all that the projection includes, but not what is projected. Therefore, though what is projected is not itself included, its possibility is.

Im Satz ist also sein Sinn noch nicht enthalten, wohl aber die Möglichkeit ihn auszudrücken.

A proposition, therefore, does not actually contain its sense, but does contain the possibility of expressing it.

("Der Inhalt des Satzes" heisst der Inhalt des sinn-vollen Satzes.)

("The content of a proposition" means the content of a proposition that has sense.)

Im Satz ist die Form seine Sinnes enthalten, aber nicht dessen Inhalt.

A proposition contains the form, but not the content of its sense.

The first two sentences are intelligible enough with '*Satz*' taken as 'proposition'; their relevance to their new context is clear. The proposition includes not only the propositional sign, but also the projecting thought; it does not include the state of affairs which is projected (if the proposition is false there is no such state of affairs for it to include) but it includes the possibility of that state of affairs (because of its pictorial form, which is the possibility that things are related to one another in the same way as the elements of the picture, 2.151). But the next sentence is hard to make sense of if '*Satz*' means proposition: commentators have tended to ignore the '*ihn auszudrücken*' at the end and taken it as if, like the previous sentence, it was saying that a proposition contained the possibility of its sense's *being the case*. But that is not at all the same as the possibility of its *expressing* its sense. But is there not something very odd about saying that a proposition contains the *possibility of expressing* its sense, when what it does is *actually to express* its sense? Everything at once becomes clear if we read '*Satz*' here as '*Satzzeichen*': a propositional sign, without the projecting thought, will not have a sense; but, being capable of being projected, it will be capable of expressing that sense. This reading also makes it possible to make sense of the puzzling parenthesis which follows. The content of the propositional sign, *when it becomes a proposition*, is its sense; the content of the sense of the proposition are the objects of the possible state of affairs which the proposition depicts; the proposition as a whole – the proposition which is propositional sign plus thought sense – contains the form but not the content of its sense: it is made up of objects which are not identical with, but formally congruent with, the objects in the possible state of affairs.

'In a proposition', Wittgenstein says at 3.2, 'a thought can be expressed in such a way that elements of the propositional sign correspond to the objects of the thought.' The expression 'the objects of the thought' is ambiguous. Does it mean: the objects which constitute the thought; or does it mean: the objects which the thought is about? One might be inclined to think the latter if one did not consult the corresponding passage in the *Prototractatus*. Between the *Prototractatus* and the *Tractatus* a passage which clearly meant the latter has been altered into one which more naturally means the former. 'The objects of the thought' will be the psychic elements whose relation to each other constitutes the thought. A proposition is fully analysed when the elements of the propositional sign correspond to the elements of the thought. An unanalysed proposition of ordinary language does not bear this relation to the thought: on the contrary, it disguises the thought; and we can understand ordinary language, we can grasp the thought beneath the folds of language, only because of enormously complicated tacit conventions (4.002). Bits of ordinary language – signs – such as the word 'is' may signify in many different ways: they belong to different symbols (3.323). What makes the difference between sign and symbol is the significant use of the sign. This goes for propositional signs too: it is the use, the application, which makes the propositional sign into the symbol, the proposition (3.320–7). The physical features of the propositional sign are those which enable it to express its sense (3.34). The most important of these is the mathematical multiplicity which is in common with the situation depicted (4.04). Normally, the propositional sign, in itself, will not have this multiplicity: if it did, it could not be said to 'disguise thought'. The multiplicity is therefore given by the tacit conventions which relate the sign and the symbol, the tacit conventions which are tantamount to the rules of logical syntax (3.334).

We may now turn to the second part of the *Tractatus* philosophy of mind: the analysis of propositions reporting belief, thought and judgment. 'It is clear', says Wittgenstein, 'that "A believes that p", "A has the thought p" and "A says p" are of the form " 'p' says p": and this does not involve a correlation of a fact with an object, but rather the correlation of facts by means of the correlation of their objects' (5.542). This comes in a passage where Wittgenstein is explaining how such propositions are not exceptions to the rule that propositions can be constructed out of other propositions only truth-functionally.

Professor Anscombe, in her *Introduction to Wittgenstein's Tractatus*, explains this passage as follows:

> . . . for anything to be capable of representing the fact that p, it must be as complex as the fact that p; but a thought that p, or a belief or statement that p, must be potentially a representation of the fact that p (and of course actually a representation of it, if it *is* a fact that p). It is perhaps not quite right to say that 'A judges p' is of the form ' "p" says that p'; what he should have said was that the business part of 'A judges that p', the part that relates to something having as its content a potential representation of the fact that p, was of the form ' "p" says that p': 'A believes p' or 'conceives p' or 'says p' must mean 'There occurs in A or is produced by A something which is (capable of being) a picture of p'.[2]

This seems correct. But Professor Anscombe goes on to say that ' "p" says that p' is offered by Wittgenstein as a possible form of

[2] G. E. M. Anscombe, *An Introduction to Wittgenstein's Tractatus* (Hutchinson, 1959), p. 88.

proposition, with true–false poles. She quotes 3.1432 ('The complex sign "*aRb*" says that *a* stands in the relation *R* to *b*'. No, not that but rather '*That* "*a*" stands to "*b*" in a certain relation says *that aRb*.') and gives as an instance of the kind of thing that Wittgenstein meant 'it is . . . the fact that "*a*" stands to the left, and "*b*" to the right of "*R*", that says that *aRb*', (p. 89).

To me it seems, on the contrary, that Wittgenstein regarded ' "*p*" says that *p*' as a pseudo-proposition.[3] It is false that it is the fact that, say, in 'London is bigger than Paris' 'London' is to the left of 'is bigger than' and 'Paris' is to the right of 'is bigger than' that *says* that London is bigger than Paris. It is only this fact *plus the conventions of the English language* that says any such thing. The description of any fact, such as Professor Anscombe mentions, which falls short of specifying those conventions in full would at best be a description of accidental features of the *Satzzeichen*. What does the saying in that sentence is what the propositional sign has in common with all other propositional signs which could achieve the same purpose; and what *this* is could only be described by – *per impossibile* – specifying and making explicit the tacit conventions of English.

' "*p*" says that *p*' does not have true–false poles. For what appears within the nested quotation marks is either – as Anscombe understands it – a description of accidental features of the propositional sign, in which case the proposition is always false; or it is a description which identifies '*p*' precisely as the proposition which says that *p*; in which case the proposition is necessarily true (and therefore, for Wittgenstein, a pseudo-proposition). But even if Anscombe were correct in thinking that ' "*p*" says that *p*' were a genuine proposition, it is difficult to see how, on her account, '*p*' does not occur non-truth-functionally in it. Whereas if ' "*p*" says that *p*' is only a pseudo-proposition, and 'A believes that "*p*" ' is of that form, it is easy to see how propositions reporting beliefs are no exception to the rule that propositions can only occur in other genuine propositions as the bases of truth-functional operations.

' "*p*" says that *p*', though a pseudo-proposition, is of course a *correct* pseudo-proposition: it is a thesis of the *Tractatus*. It is shown

---

[3] Cf. A. Kenny, *Wittgenstein* (Allen Lane/Penguin Press, 1973), p. 101.

by the proposition 'p': (4.022, 4.462). This alone suffices to show that it cannot be *said* for what can be shown cannot be said; and anything that attempts to say what can only be shown is a pseudo-proposition (4.1212).

We are now in a better position to see in what way the philosophy of psychology clarifies psychological propositions. Suppose that I think a certain thought: my thinking that thought will consist in certain psychic elements – mental images or internal impressions, perhaps – standing in a relation to each other. That these elements stand in such and such a relation will be a psychological fact; a fact in the world, within the purview of the natural sciences; just as the fact that the penholder is on the table is a physical fact within the purview of the natural sciences. But the fact that these mental elements have the meaning they have will not be a fact of science, any more than the fact (if it is a fact) that the penholder's being on the table says that the cat is on the mat (if the appropriate code is in force).

Meaning is conferred on signs by *us*, by our conventions (3.3, 3.322, 3.342, 4.026, 6.53, etc.). But where are the acts of the will that confer the meaning, that set up the conventions? They cannot be in the empirical soul studied by superficial psychology: any relation between *that* will and any pair of objects would be a fact in the world, capable of study by natural science, and therefore incapable of the ineffable activity of conferring meaning. When I confer meaning on the symbols I use, the I that does so must be the metaphysical I, not the self that is studied by psychology (5.631ff).

There is a tension between the 5.541s as I have explained them and the 3s as Wittgenstein explained them to Russell. From the 5.541s it seems as if what gives meaning to the perceptible signs of language cannot be anything psychic. From the 3s it seems as though the projection lines between the propositional sign and the world are drawn in the realm of psychology: it is thinking which constructs the sense of the proposition. But perhaps the *Tractatus* philosophy of mind is easy to make consistent: we need only to draw in the 3s a distinction suggested by our reflections on the 5.54s. In the thought itself, perhaps, we can distinguish between the particular mental configuration, studiable by psychology, and the significance or intentionality of that configuration, conferred by the metaphysical self. Thought, unlike language, will have the right mathematical multiplicity to depict the facts; but is multiplicity gives it only the *possibility* of depicting; that it actually does depict depends on the meaning of its elements, and that is given by the extra-psychological will giving those elements a use, an application.

The later Wittgenstein came to believe that it was absurd to look for a multiplicity of mental items in independence from the mulitplicity of their expression. For this reason he could jeer at the idea that things were possible in the mysterious medium of the mind which were impossible in the public light of day. The *Tractatus* may perhaps have conceived thought as a gaseous medium: but if I am right it did *not* think that thought – the realm of introspectionist psychology – could confer meaning. The constant later polemic against the imagist theory of meaning goes further than the *Tractatus* in that it argued that even images are only identifiable as the images they are in virtue of the meaning we attach to them. But the *Tractatus* itself did not think, as the British empiricists did, that impressions and ideas could themselves confer meaning unaided. In the *Tractatus* meaning is conferred by pure will, the pure will of the extra-mundane solipsistic metaphysical self; in the *Philosophical Investigations* it is conferred by the active participation of the human being in the social community in the empirical world. From one point of view the two conceptions could hardly be further apart. But common to both are two theses of fundamental importance: first, that introspectionist psychology can never explain meaning; secondly, that the ultimate creation of meaning is indescribable (in the *Tractatus*, because it takes place outside the world; in the *Philosophical Investigations*, because all description is within a language-game). And common to both are the tasks and method of philosophy of mind: to clarify psychological statements by separating out the logical and intentional from the contingent and empirical.

2

The Ghost of the *Tractatus*

Wittengenstein was unreliable as an historian of philosophy. When he criticized other philosophers he rarely gave chapter and verse for his criticism, and on the rare occasions on which he quoted verbatim he did not always do justice to the authors quoted. I will illustrate this first in the comparatively unimportant case of Augustine and then in the more serious case of Frege.

The *Philosophical Investigations* begins with a quotation from St Augustine's Confessions. Ever since the early thirties Wittgenstein had taken Augustine as the spokesman for a certain view of language: the view that naming is the foundation of language and that the meaning of a word is the object for which it stands (*Philosophische Grammatik*, pp. 56–7). The passage quoted in the *Investigations* lays great stress on the role of ostension in the learning of words, and makes no distinction between different parts of speech (*PI*, I, §1). Despite this, Augustine is a curious choice as a spokesman for the views which Wittgenstein attacks since in many respects what he says resembles Wittgenstein's own views rather than the views that are Wittgenstein's target.

In the early pages of the *Investigations* Wittgenstein is concerned to argue that ostensive definition cannot have the fundamental role sometimes assigned to it in the learning of language because (a) the understanding of an ostension presupposes a certain mastery of language and (b) ostension by itself cannot make clear the role which the word to be defined is to have in language. Both these are points with which Augustine agreed. As a presupposition of the parents being able to show objects to the child, he mentions that they express their intentions 'by the bodily movements, as it were the natural language of all peoples'. In saying this he is not saying that a child 'already has a language, only not this one' (*PI*, I, §32);

he is drawing attention to a point often made by Wittgenstein, that the setting up of linguistic conventions presupposes a uniformity among human beings in their natural, pre-conventional, reactions to such things as pointing fingers (*PG*, p. 94; *PI*, I, §185). Again, Augustine does not think that the ostension by itself will teach the child the meaning of the word: the child must also 'hear the words repeatedly used in their proper places in various sentences' (*PI*, I, §1).

For Augustine the beginning of the whole learning process is the child's own efforts to express its sensations and needs prelinguistically: just before the passage quoted by Wittgenstein he says: 'By cries and various sounds and movements of my limbs I tried to express my inner feelings and get my will obeyed'.[1] Thus he agrees with Wittgenstein that 'words are connected with the primitive, the natural, expressions of the sensation and used in their place' (*PI*, I, §244). Augustine clearly distinguishes between this natural expression (for which he uses the verbs *edere, aperire, indicare*) and the relation between a word and what it signifies (for which he uses expressions involving the root *sign-* and the verb *enuntiare*). Finally, it is worth remarking that this spokesman for the name-theory nowhere uses the word *nomen* in this passage, and calls words *signa voluntatum* as often as he calls them *signa rerum*.

The misrepresentation of Augustine was not due to any hostility on Wittgenstein's part. On the contrary, a number of Wittgenstein's friends have recorded that he regarded Augustine as a great man and a clear thinker. What this shows is that even great admiration for a thinker did not ensure that Wittgenstein would represent him accurately.

This is much more obvious and much more serious in Wittgenstein's treatment of 'the great works of Frege'. In the *Tractatus* Frege is referred to in fifteen passages: in at least five of these he is misrepresented. I will illustrate this briefly.

(1) At 3.143 Wittgenstein says that Frege was able to call a proposition a composite name because of the obscuring effect of the way we write things, which means that no difference appears in print between a sentence and a word. This had nothing to do with

---

[1] *Confessions*, 1, 8: *cum gemitibus et vocibus variis et variis membrorum motibus, edere vellem sensa cordis mei, ut voluntati paretur.*

Frege's reasons for calling a proposition a name.[2] In an ordinary arithmetic textbook, an equation looks exactly the same whether it is used to make a statement or only as the expression of an assumption: according to Frege it is a name in the latter case but not in the former (GB, p. 34n).

(2) At 4.063 Wittgenstein says that Frege thought that the verb of a proposition was '. . . is true' or '. . . is false'. In the *Begriffschrift* Frege thought that the verb of a proposition was '. . . is true', but he soon abandoned this view, which was inconsistent with other things he said in that work; and at no time of his life did he think that the verb of a proposition was '. . . is false'.[3]

(3) At 5.02 Wittgenstein accuses Frege of having confused argument and index. Max Black comments on this passage. 'Wittgenstein's allegation is incorrect. Had Frege really thought of the names composing a proposition as "indices" in Wittgenstein's sense, he must have conceded that the meaning of a proposition could just as well have been conveyed by a simple symbol – say T for a true proposition and F for a false one. Now Frege would have agreed that the reference (*Bedeutung*) of a proposition could be identified by a name; but he also held that the sense of a proposition was a function of the senses of its components (as Wittgenstein himself seems to recognize at 3.318 in his allusion to Frege).'[4]

(4) At 5.521 Wittgenstein says that Frege 'introduced generality in association with logical product or logical sum'. There is no warrant for this in the way Frege introduces generality e.g. in *Function and Concept* (GB, p. 35).

(5) At 6.1271 Wittgenstein makes the proposal that one might derive logic from the logical product of Frege's primitive proposition. He goes on: 'Frege would perhaps say that we should then no longer have an immediately self-evident primitive proposition. But it is remarkable that a thinker as rigorous as Frege appealed to the

[2] *Translations from the Philosophical Writings of Gottlob Frege*, ed. Peter Geach and Max Black (Blackwell, 1960) (hereafter GB), p. 63.
[3] Cf. G. E. M. Anscombe, *An Introduction to Wittgenstein's Tractatus* (Hutchinson, 1959), p. 106.
[4] Max Black, *A Companion to Wittgenstein's Tractatus* (Cambridge University Press, 1964), p. 239.

degree of self-evidence as the criterion of a logical proposition.' One cannot help noticing how within the space of a sentence a counterfactual has changed into a categorical, and how Frege is taken to task for something which has been put into his mouth by Wittgenstein. Black comments, 'This seems unfair to Frege and especially to his sharp separation of logical from psychological considerations. Frege held "that arithmetic is a branch of logic and need not borrow any ground of proof whatever from experience or intuition"' (GB, p. 148). Frege does sometimes talk of self-evidence, as when commenting on the difficulties created by Russell's paradox for Axiom V of the *Grundgesetze*: 'I have never disguised from myself its lack of the self-evidence that belongs to the other axioms and that must properly be demanded of a logical law' (GB, p. 234). So Black's defence of Frege is perhaps too generous. Still, if Frege sometimes talks of self-evidence, so does Wittgenstein – when criticizing Frege! (e.g. 5.42: 'It is self-evident that ∨, ⊃, etc. are not relations in the sense in which right and left etc. are relations.')

The unfairness of some of Wittgenstein's criticism of Frege is no doubt partially to be explained by the inaccuracy of the account of Frege in the appendix to Russell's *Principles of Mathematics* on which Wittgenstein seems sometimes to have relied.

I draw attention to Wittgenstein's treatment of Augustine and Frege because I want to suggest that his carelessness as a critic affected not only his discussion of his admired predecessors but also his later polemic against his own early work. I wish to claim that his own later statements about the *Tractatus* sometimes misrepresent it and mask the considerable continuity between his later views and his earlier ones. In particular, I shall try to show that he came to misrepresent the *Tractatus* on the nature of names, on the nature of objects, on the nature of facts, and on the nature of propositions. If I can make out my case, one upshot will be that Wittgenstein will be shown to have overestimated in later life the distance which separated the picture theory of meaning from the discussions of meaning in the *Philosophical Investigations*. This should not surprise us. As an epigraph to the *Investigations* Wittgenstein sapiently placed a quotation from Nestroy: 'It is in the nature of every advance, that it appears much greater than it actually is.'

From the early thirties onwards Wittgenstein thought it important
not to identify the meaning of a name with its bearer, the object for
which it stood. He also thought that it was erroneous to suggest
that acquaintance with the bearer of a name was sufficient for
knowledge of the meaning of a name; and hence, as we saw earlier,
he attacked the primacy of ostensive definition in language learning. How far do these later attacks bear on the doctrine of the
Tractatus?

There seems no doubt that the *Tractatus* identifies the meaning of
a word with its bearer: 3.203: 'A name means an object. The object
is its meaning.' And in conversation with Waismann in July 1932,
having said that ostensive definition remains within language and
does not involve any confrontation between sign and reality, he
went on to say 'When I wrote the *Tractatus* I was unclear about
logical analysis and ostensive definition. I then thought that there
is a "linking up of language with reality".'[5]

At *Tractatus*, 2.1513–4 Wittgenstein says that the correlations
between the elements of a picture and things in the world are 'as it
were the feelers of the picture's elements, with which the picture
touches reality'. However, it is not said that the correlation is made
by ostensive definition. 'Ostensive definition' does not appear in
the index to the *Tractatus*, but that is unsurprising since the
expression was not yet in use as a technical term. (I owe this point
to Dr P. Hacker.) But no other term appears which could be a
non-technical equivalent. *Hindeuten* and *hinweisen* appear in 5.461,
2.02331, 5.02, 5.522, but not in the appropriate sense. The nearest
to an allusion to ostensive definition is the passage at 3.263: 'The
meanings of primitive signs (*die Bedeutungen von Urzeichen*) can be
explained by means of elucidations. Elucidations are propositions
that contain the primitive signs. So they can only be understood if
the meanings of those signs are already known.'

Max Black finds this passage 'disturbing'. On Wittgenstein's
view, he says, 'It is impossible to explain a name's meaning
explicitly: the only way to convey the meaning is to use the name in

[5] F. Waismann, *Ludwig Wittgenstein and the Vienna Circle* (Blackwell, 1979), pp. 209–10.

a proposition, thus presupposing that the meaning is already understood. On this view, the achievement of common reference by speaker and bearer becomes mysterious' (*Companion*, p. 115). No more mysterious, one might think, than artificial respiration; but our concern is not with the plausibility of the view, but with its relationship to the *Investigations* criticism of ostensive definition.

One thing which Wittgenstein is very clearly *not* saying in 3.263 is that first we learn the meanings of names by ostensive definition, and then when we have hooked the names on to the world, we can put them together into sentences. Nor is he saying that before understanding propositions you have to understand the names that occur in them, and before understanding names you have to understand the propositions in which they occur. That would indeed make the learning of meaning mysterious and inexplicable. What he is saying is that the understanding of names and the understanding of propositions stand or fall together. And of course that is what you would expect the *Tractatus* to say in view of its claim that it is only in the context of a proposition that a name *has* a meaning (3.3).

What is clear in both the *Tractatus* and the *Investigations* is that you can't learn the meaning of a name in isolation from its use (which is, *inter alia*, the way it fits into propositions). The *Investigations*, so far from contradicting, takes a stage further the *Tractatus* point that one cannot think of the meaning of propositions and the meaning of names as two separate lessons to be mastered in the course of coming to understand language. It points out that in very primitive cases of linguistic understanding it may not even be possible to identify names and propositions as separable elements of language (*PI*, I, §§9–20). The *Tractatus*, so far from saying that it is acquaintance with the bearers of names which hooks the propositions on to the world, insists that the only way in which the primitive signs themselves can be understood is by using them in full-blown propositions. Certainly, Wittgenstein thought at that time that *the way in which* the use of names in propositions communicated their reference to others was a matter for empirical psychology, whereas later he thought it was part of the subject-matter of philosophy; but this extension of the realm of philosophy did not itself involve any going back on the theses which were already recognized as philosophical at the time of the *Tractatus*.

A passage in the *Philosophische Bemerkungen* makes quite clear that the ostensive definitions which don't take us beyond language are different from the elucidating propositions of the *Tractatus*.

> If I explain the meaning of a word 'A' to someone by pointing to something and saying 'this is A', this expression may be meant in two different ways. Either it is itself a proposition, in which case it can only be understood if the meaning of A is already known, i.e. I must leave it to chance whether or not he understands the sentence as I mean it; or it is a definition. Suppose I have said to someone 'A is ill', but he doesn't know who I mean by 'A', and I now point at a man, saying 'this is A'. Here the expression is a definition, but this can only be understood if he has already gathered the kind of object it is through his understanding of the grammar of the proposition 'A is ill'. But this means that any kind of explanation of a language presupposes a language already. (*PB*, p. 54)

Here it is the 'this is A' meant as a proposition, or 'A is ill', which would be elucidations in the sense of the *Tractatus*. 'This is A' meant in the second way is the ostensive definition which might wrongly be thought to take one outside language and presuppose nothing linguistic. The criticism of the role assigned to ostensive definition quite passes by the account briefly given in the *Tractatus*.

THE NATURE OF OBJECTS

Students of the *Tractatus* disagree whether that work is to be taken in a nominalist or Platonist sense: whether, that is to say, the objects which form the fixed substance of the world are to be interpreted as individuals (such as the material particles of physics) or as universals (such as the colour red or the property of tiredness). The *Notebooks* that precede the *Tractatus* show that Wittgenstein himself veered between nominalist and Platonist positions, and provide to that extent support for the rival interpretations of the *Tractatus*. However, it seems to me no accident that it is difficult to decide the question from the study of the *Tractatus* alone; when writing the book Wittgenstein chose his words carefully so as not to adopt either of the positions about which the *Notebooks* express his doubts and hesitations.

The conversations with Waismann contain a very interesting passage dated 22 December 1929. Wittgenstein was discussing the nature of objects as conceived by Frege and Russell and the possibility of representing all colour statements by means of an apparatus like the colour octahedron.

If the four primary colours would be adequate for this purpose, he said, they could be called 'elements of representation', and it is these elements of representation that are the 'objects'. 'It makes no sense to ask whether the objects are something thing-like, whether they are something that stands in the subject place, or are something like a property, or are relations and so on' (Waismann, p. 43). This thought is continuous with the one expressed in the *Philosophical Investigations* (*PI*, I, §50): 'What looks as if it had to exist [what has been discussed is the nature of objects in the *Tractatus* (*PI*, I, §46)] is part of our language. It is a paradigm in our language-game: something with which comparison is made. And this may be an important observation; but it is none the less an observation concerning our language-game – our method of representation.'

In the conversations with Waismann, as in the *Tractatus*, Wittgenstein refuses to adopt either the Platonist or the nominalist notion of objects; but commonly in the thirties he writes as if the objects of the *Tractatus* had been like Platonic Ideas. A striking case in an unexpected context occurs in the 1931 *Remarks on the Golden Bough*: 'To cast out death or slay death; but he is also represented as a skeleton, as in some sense dead himself. "As dead as death." "Nothing is so dead as death; nothing is so beautiful as beauty itself." Here the image which we use in thinking of reality is that beauty, death etc. are the pure (concentrated) substances, and they are found in the beautiful object as added ingredients of the mixture. – And do I not recognize here my own observations on "object" and "complex"?' (*The Human World*, 3, p. 36).

In an essay which now appears as an appendix to the *Philosophische Grammatik* there is a discussion of objects which begins with the quotation 'An object cannot, in a certain sense, be described'. That seems to be an allusion to *Tractatus*, 3.221: 'Objects can only be *named*. Signs are their representatives. I can only speak *about* them; I cannot put them into words. Propositions

can only say how things are, not what they are.' There follows an
allusion to Plato's *Theaetetus* (201E) and the remark 'By description
is meant "definition". For it is naturally not denied that the object
can "be described from the outside", that say properties can be
ascribed to it'. That may well be true of the *Tractatus*, but it is not
true of Plato: in Socrates' dream in the *Theatetus* it really is being
denied that any true predications can be made of the elements. But
no matter, our concern is not with Wittgenstein's exegesis of Plato,
but Wittgenstein's exegesis of Wittgenstein. For this purpose the
most interesting feature of the passage is that the examples it takes
of objects are colours considered as universals, the colours blue and
red, the references of the names 'blue' and 'red' considered as
undefinable signs. The passage ends by saying 'If you call the
colour green an object you must say that this object occurs in a
symbolism. Otherwise the sense of the symbolism, and therefore its
being a symbolism, would not be guaranteed' (*PG*, p. 209).

This passage too fits well with the discussion in the *Investigations*
where Wittgenstein imagines samples of colour being preserved in
Paris like the standard metre, so that one can define, e.g. 'sepia' as
the colour of the standard sepia kept hermetically sealed there.
Such a sample will be not something represented, but a means of
representation (*PI*, I, §50). But again the *Tractatus* is being
misrepresented, for in that work it is said explicitly that colours are
not simple objects, since colours have a logical structure which
explains the impossibility of the simultaneous presence of two
colours at the same place in the visual field (6.3751).

FACT AND COMPLEX

The most interesting of the later criticisms of the *Tractatus* is
contained in an essay of 1931 entitled 'Komplex und Tatsache'
which appears as an appendix both to the *Philosophische Bemerkungen*
and to the *Philosophische Grammatik*. I will quote the crucial part, in
Roger White's translation.

> Complex is not like fact. For I can e.g. say of a complex that it
> moves from one place to another, but not of a fact.
> But that this complex is now situated here is a fact.

'This complex of buildings is coming down' is tantamount to: 'The buildings thus grouped together are coming down'.

I call a flower, a house, a constellation complexes: moreover, complexes of petals, bricks, stars, etc.

That this constellation is located here, can of course be described by a proposition in which only its stars are mentioned and neither the word 'constellation' nor its name occurs.

But that is all there is to say about the relation between complex and fact. And a complex is a spatial object, composed of spatial objects. (The concept 'spatial' admitting of a certain extension.)

A complex is composed of its parts, the things of a kind which go to make it up. (This is of course a grammatical proposition concerning the words 'complex', 'part' and 'compose'.)

To say that a red circle is composed of redness and circularity, or is a complex with these component parts, is a misuse of these words and is misleading. (Frege was aware of this and told me it.)

It is just as misleading to say the fact that this circle is red (that I am tired) is a complex whose component parts are a circle and redness (myself and tiredness). (*PG*, pp. 199–200)

This passage is surprising in various ways. It suggests that Wittgenstein once held the view that a fact was a complex of objects, and that he was cured of this erroneous view by reflection on a remark of Frege's. But in fact in the years before the *Tractatus* Wittgenstein constantly attacks the idea that a proposition like 'this circle is red' stands for a complex, and (rightly or wrongly) attaches part of the blame for that erroneous idea to Frege. For instance, in the 1913 *Notes on Logic*: 'Frege said "propositions are names": Russell said "propositions correspond to complexes". Both are false; and especially false is the statement "propositions are names of complexes". Facts cannot be names' (*NB*, p. 93; cf. *Tractatus*, 3.144). And the *Tractatus*, though it speaks of objects as constituents (*Bestandteile*) of states of affairs, and states of affairs as concatenations of objects (2.01) never says that a fact is a complex of objects, or commits itself to the existence of Platonic objects like redness and tiredness. Indeed it contains an attack on Frege for confusing (in the case of the proposition) a complex with a fact (3.143).

The contrast is so striking that one casts about for a different way of reading the passage. Is this really a criticism of the *Tractatus* at all? Does the sentence 'Frege was aware of this and told me it' perhaps mean, not that it was Frege who first brought the matter to Wittgenstein's attention, but that Frege, in spite of Wittgenstein's accusations, had been aware of this all along and told Wittgenstein so (i.e. told Wittgenstein that he had), more by way of self-defence than of imparting instruction?

I do not think we can take these ways out. Various parallel passages make clear that this is an attack on the *Tractatus*. For instance, on p. 58 of the *Grammatik* we read:

> It is possible to speak perfectly intelligibly of combinations of colours and shapes (e.g. of the colours red and blue and the shapes square and circle) just as we speak of combinations of different shapes or spatial objects. And this is the origin of the bad form of expression: the fact is a complex of objects. In this the fact that a man is sick is compared with a combination of two things, one of them the man and the other the sickness.

An earlier version of this passage is more explicit: instead of '*des schlechten Ausdrucks*' it reads '*meines irreleitenden Ausdrucks*': *my* misleading expression: the fact is a complex of objects. In the *Blue Book*, p. 31 we are told: 'We are misled by the substantives "object of thought" and "fact" and by the different meanings of the word "exist". Talking of the fact as a "complex of objects" springs from this confusion (cf. *Tractatus Logico-Philosophicus*).' Peter Geach records that Wittgenstein told him that after reading the *Tractatus* Frege asked him whether a fact was larger than an object which was a constituent of it. In the essay 'Complex and Fact' we read: 'The part smaller than the whole. Applied to fact and constituent that would give an absurdity' (*PG*, p. 201).

There seems no doubt then that Wittgenstein meant the strictures of the essay to apply to the *Tractatus*. One of the strictures gets home. *Tractatus*, 5.5423 says: 'To perceive a complex means to perceive that its constituents are related to one another in such and such a way.' *PG*, p. 200 says: 'We also say "to point out a fact", but that always means: "to point out the fact that . . ." Whereas "to point at (or point out) a flower" doesn't mean to point out that this blossom is on this stalk; for we needn't be talking about this blossom and this stalk at all.' This is a fair point. It anticipates the well-known passage about the broomstick and the broom in the *Investigations* (*PI*, I, §60). But here and in the *Investigations* what is in question is not facts considered as complexes, but complexes considered as facts: Wittgenstein is saying (correctly) that spatial complexes are not the same as the fact of the existence of the spatial complexes. But it is quite a different thing to claim that a fact is itself a complex of objects. This is the claim the essay principally attacks, and this is the one that it is unfair to saddle the *Tractatus* with.

The unfairness consists principally in ignoring the distinction made in the *Tractatus* between *Tatsache* (fact) and *Sachverhalt* (state of affairs). In the *Tractatus* Wittgenstein wrote:

> In a state of affairs objects fit into one another like the links of a chain. In a state of affairs objects stand in a determinate relation to one another. (2.03, 031)

In the *Grammatik* he takes up this metaphor to criticize it:

> A chain is composed of its links, not of these and their spatial relations. The fact that these links are so concatenated isn't *composed* of anything at all. (*PG*, p. 201)

But in the *Tractatus*, too, the fact that the links were concatenated (whether literal links in a literal chain, or objects in a state of affairs) would be a fact, the *existence* of a *Sachverhalt*, and that too would not be composed of anything. The *Grammatik* insists that there is an important difference between the complex consisting of *a*-standing-in-the-relation-*R*-to-*b* and the fact that *a* stands in the relation *R* to *b*. In the *Tractatus* at 3.1432 that distinction is already drawn with complete sharpness and given an important place in the theory of the proposition.

THE PICTURE THEORY

It is commonly said that Wittgenstein after the *Tractatus* abandoned the picture theory of the proposition. He certainly came to regard it as incomplete, and he certainly came to think that he had misconceived the relation between thought and proposition. In the *Tractatus* he regarded the thought as a ghostly intermediary between sentence and fact, where, in the ghostly medium of the mind, the projection lines were drawn between the proposition and what it represented (3.11). He later came to think that it was language which linked thought to reality, not the other way round; and he came to think that no lines of projection could do what the *Tractatus* thought was supposed to do (*PG*, p. 214).

In my book *Wittgenstein* I have argued that it is a mistake to overestimate the philosopher's change of mind with regard to the picture theory. Many of the logical features of the theory, I have argued, survived with more or less modification the abandonment of the atomism of the *Tractatus*. I do not wish to repeat here what I have written elsewhere: instead I will single out one feature of the picture theory which remained influential throughout Wittgenstein's life: the bipolarity of the proposition. Any proposition which *can* be true, Wittgenstein insisted from 1913 onwards, *can* be false. This thesis, which is a crucial element of the picture theory, is tantamount to the thesis that there are only contingent propositions. If every genuine proposition is capable of being false, then there are no necessary truths: synthetic *a priori* truths are impossible and analytic truths are 'propositions' only by courtesy. The thesis of bipolarity is constantly reaffirmed throughout Wittgenstein's life: in the conversations with Waismann (pp. 67, 88, 97), in the *Philosophische Grammatik* (p. 129), in the *Blue Book* (p. 54), in the *Philosophical Investigations* (I, §251). It is tantamount to the insistence that what gives a proposition its sense must be independent of what gives it its truth, which is also a notion which recurs from the early *Notebooks* (p. 107) through *Bemerkungen* (*PB*, p. 78) into the argument against private languages in the *Investigations*.

Even the isomorphism between the world and language survives, though with its poles reversed, in the later philosophy. Dr Hacker has put it neatly in his book *Insight and Illusion*: 'In the *Investigations* the structure of language . . . is still isomorphic with the structure of reality, not because language must mirror the logical form of the universe, but because the apparent "structure of reality" is merely the shadow of grammar.' Whichever way it is facing, the isomorphism has the effect that the structure of reality can only be shown not described, and that the structure of language cannot be justified.

The first entry in the *Notebook* is 'logic must take care of itself'. That is an abiding thought of Wittgenstein's philosophy. Throughout his life he continued to deny that philosophy could provide a justification for logic, or as he would later call it, grammar, or language games. One of the clearest passages about this is in the *Philosophische Grammatik*, which stands in the middle of his life firmly anchoring the earlier to the later philosophy.

> The rules of grammar cannot be justified by shewing that their application makes a representation agree with reality. For these justifications must themselves describe what is represented. And if something can be said in those justifications and is permitted by their grammar – why shouldn't it be also permitted by the grammar that I am trying to justify? Why shouldn't both forms of expression have the same freedom? And how could what the one says restrict what the other can say? (*PG*, p. 186)

He might have said at the end of the *Investigations*, about attempts to justify grammar, what he said at the end of the *Tractatus*: whereof one cannot speak thereof one must be silent. Instead, if one had to choose an epigram to end his later work, one might choose something which expresses the same thought, but in a more tolerant vein: a thought which he attributes to St Augustine but which, like the theory of language with which the *Investigations* began, is difficult to locate in the actual text of the Saint.

Was, du Mistviech, du willst keinen Unsinn reden? Rede nur einen Unsinn, es macht nichts! (Waismann, p. 123)

3

From the Big Typescript to the
Philosophical Grammar

The Special Supplement which G. H. von Wright contributed in
October 1969 to the *Philosophical Review* (vol. 78, pp. 483–503) on
the Wittgenstein Papers remains a most valuable tool for anyone
who wishes to follow Wittgenstein's development or investigate the
history of his published works. In addition to the definitive
catalogue of the papers it contains a wealth of information in a
lucid and economical form about the origin, discovery, and actual
or planned publication of Wittgenstein's literary remains. Item 213
in von Wright's list reads 'The so-called Big Typescript. Probably
1933. viii+768pp.' In discussing the literary executors' publication
plans von Wright wrote:

> A ... complicated case was presented by the so-called Big Type-
> script of 1933 ... This last third of it, on the philosophy of
> mathematics, was evidently relatively finished even in the author's
> opinion. But on the first two-thirds Wittgenstein had started to
> make extensive revisions. The revisions were first made in the
> typescript, but the work was continued in new manuscripts from the
> years 1933 and 1934. Eventually there existed something which can
> be called a new manuscript version of these parts of the Big
> Typescript, and it seemed best to publish this *manuscript* with the
> concluding third part of the *typescript*. The work will appear in two
> volumes under the title *Philosophische Grammatik*. (p. 502)

The German text of the *Philosophische Grammatik*, edited by Rush
Rhees, in fact appeared in a single volume in 1969. Later, I made
an English version of the Rhees edition, which was published in
1974. In the course of working on the translation and consulting the

Wittgenstein manuscripts for help in understanding difficult passages, I became aware that the preparation of the *Philosophische Grammatik* for publication had involved a more substantial degree of editorial intervention than is immediately apparent from the *Anmerkung des Herausgebers* appended to it. The present essay is meant to supplement, for readers of the *Philosophical Grammar*, the information about its history contained in von Wright's article and Rhees' note.

'In an outward sense', von Wright wrote of the Big Typescript, 'it is perhaps the most finished of all Wittgenstein's writings after the *Tractatus*.' Though it bore no title, it was divided into chapters and section, each with its own title, and it was preceded by an eight page table of contents. Other papers in the *Nachlass* enable us to study its origin. Wittgenstein was in the habit of noting down philosophical remarks in manuscript volumes, often in dated entries in a manner familiar to readers of his posthumously published *Notebooks 1914–1916*. To these volumes he gave roman numerals, and often a title. The volumes from the period August 1930 until December 1933 bear the following numbers and titles:

Volume IV. '*Philosophische Bemerkungen.*' 13 December 1929 – August 1930 (VW 108).

Volume V. '*Bemerkungen.*' 11 August 1930 – 3 February 1931 (VW 109).

Volume VI. '*Philosophische Bemerkungen.*' 10 December 1930 – 6 July 1931 (VW 110).

Volume VII. '*Bemerkungen zur Philosophie.*' 7 July–September 1931 (VW 111).

Volume VIII. '*Bemerkungen zur philosophischen Grammatik.*' 5 October – 28 November 1931 (VW 112).

Volume IX. '*Philosophische Grammatik.*' 28 November 1931 – 23 May 1932 (VW 113).

Volume X. '*Philosophische Grammatik.*' First entry 27 May 1932 (VW 114).

Volume XI. '*Philosophische Bemerkungen.*' First entry 14 December 1933 (VW 115).

From manuscript notebooks of this kind Wittgenstein dictated to typists, revising, re-ordering and freshly composing in the course of dictation. One such typescript was based on the second half of volume IV; another on volumes V–IX and the beginning of volume X. Together, the two made up some 850 pages (VW 210, 211). He cut up a copy of these typed texts into fragments (*Zettel*) so that he could rearrange the order of the remarks and group them into sections. There exists a rearrangement of cuttings from these typescripts and earlier material clipped together into sections and chapters and enclosed in folders. The Big Typescript is a typed fair copy of this arrangement following the grouping into chapters and sections.

It is clear that Wittgenstein at this time thought of himself as working on a book for publication. 'Philosophical Grammar' is suggested as a title for the book in a manuscript note of June 1931, and the expression was used in the titles of manuscript volumes VIII to X. The Big Typescript clearly marks a very important stage in the preparation of this book. But it is in many ways incomplete, and it is unlikely that Wittgenstein regarded it as almost ready to go to press. Certainly, as we shall see, he soon began to rearrange and rewrite its contents.

The Big Typescript consists of nineteen chapters, titled as follows. (I have added numbers to facilitate later reference.)

1. Verstehen.
2. Bedeutung.
3. Satz, Sinn des Satzes.
4. Augenblickliches Verstehen etc.
5. Wesen der Sprache.
6. Gedanke, Denken.
7. Grammatik.
8. Intention und Abbildung.
9. Logischer Schluss.
10. Allgemeinheit.
11. Erwartung, Wunsch etc.
12. Philosophie.
13. Phänomenologie.
14. Idealismus, etc.
15. Grundlagen der Mathematik.
16. Ueber Kardinalzahlen.
17. Mathematischer Beweis.

18. Induktionsbeweis. Periodizität.
19. Das Unendliche in der Mathematik.

Each of these nineteen chapters is divided into smaller sections, numbered by Wittgenstein consecutively throughout the work from 1 to 140 and headed by a title or slogan. Thus, the first chapter on understanding consists of six sections with headings such as 'Understanding, meaning, drops out of our consideration', 'Interpretation. Do we interpret every sign?' and 'Understanding as the correlate of an explanation'. The style of Wittgenstein's titles, and the general appearance of his table of contents, can be seen on pp. 31–5 of the *Philosophical Grammar*, where the latter part of it is reproduced.

The philosophical content of the Big Typescript corresponds broadly to that of the published *Philosophical Grammar*. The chapter on understanding covers the same ground, often in the same words, as the first chapter and the first half of the second chapter in the *Philosophical Grammar* (where the chapter divisions are Rhees'). The second chapter, on meaning, discusses the primitive 'Augustinian' notion of meaning, the notion of meaning as place in grammatical space, the possibility of distinguishing between primary and secondary signs and other topics treated in the second half of chapter two of the *Philosophical Grammar*. The third chapter, whose title ('The proposition and its sense') was used by Rhees as the title for the whole first part of the *Philosophical Grammar*, corresponds in the main to chapter six of that work, attacking the notion that the sense of a proposition is a soul, or that the propositions dealt with by logic are something different from the sentences of everyday life, discussing the way in which grammar determines what makes sense, working out and modifying the analogy between a proposition and a picture, analysing the concept of 'correspondence with reality'. Sections 28, 31, 32, 33, 34 of this chapter – dealing with elementary propositions, with the way in which time enters into propositions, with the nature of hypotheses, with probability, and with the concept 'about' – were published as appendices 4A, 5, 6, 7 and 8 in the *Grammar*.

The comparatively brief fourth chapter of the Big Typescript, on the relation between understanding in a flash and the grasp of rules determining meaning over time, contains material incorporated in the first chapter of the *Grammar*. The ideas of the chapter on the nature of language – the discussion of the way in which ostensive definition works, the criticism of the idea that language is a causally operating mechanism to achieve a pre-established goal, for instance – are found scattered in several places in the *Grammar*, in chapters three, five and ten. The topics of chapter six ('Thought and Thinking'), by contrast, correspond very closely to those of chapter five of the *Grammar*: thinking has no mechanism, nor does it exist to serve a purpose; it is not a mental process perhaps capable of replacement by an inorganic process; the way in which thought is localized, and the relation between thought and its expression. Several parts of the chapter on grammar seem to be closer to familiar sections of the *Philosophical Investigations* (the discussion of existence, and of the sense in which logic is normative) than to anything in the published *Grammar*: but the denial that grammar is accountable to reality corresponds to its chapter ten. The discussion of copying, rules of projection, and the connection between thoughts and their objects in chapter eight of the Big Typescript correspond to the fourth chapter of the *Grammar*.

The ninth and tenth chapters of the Big Typescript, on inference and on generality, are the first of those which are printed verbatim in the published *Grammar*. Chapters fifteen to nineteen, on the foundations of mathematics, the nature of number and of proof in mathematics, are also to be found in the published version in almost exactly the form in which they appear in the typescript. In these chapters editor's intervention has been restricted to choosing between alternative formulations which were left open by Wittgenstein, to inserting diagrams from the manuscript notebooks into the blanks left in the typescript, and to modifying the often erratic symbolism of the typescript in the light of Wittgenstein's own manuscript usage. The published text gives no indication of this editorial activity, and one can very well understand why. To have noted each editorial decision would have been to cumber the text with a mass of mainly useless information. The choices between alternatives almost always affect only the style and not the sense. (In the first section of the chapter on the foundations of mathematics some seventy words of the text are the result of editorial choice between Wittgenstein's alternatives: some 3 per cent of the total text.) Perhaps occasionally to record the rejected alternative would have thrown light on the sense of the chosen alternative. Occasionally the editor has assisted the reader to understand difficult passages of the typescript by incorporating, as explicit appendices, passages from corresponding sections of the notebooks. (E.g. *PG*, pp. 408–46.)

Between the chapter on generality and the chapter on the foundations of mathematics the Big Typescript contains four chapters which do not appear in the published version. The first of these ('Expectation and Wishing') criticizes the Russellian theory of satisfaction and develops the notion that expectations, wishes, intentions make contact with their fulfilments via their expression in language. In this it is close to chapter VII of the *Grammar*, though it also contains a treatment of belief and its grounds which is closer to sections 447f of *Philosophical Investigations*, part I.

The remaining three chapters correspond to nothing in the published *Grammar*. The chapter on philosophy offers a series of vivid metaphors for philosophical method: the philosopher is trying to get a hair off his tongue, to find the word which will unlock the combination, to destroy the idols whose myths are embedded in our speech, to hang warning signs on misleading tracks in the forest of language. Wittgenstein wants to teach philosophers patience, to stop them throwing all the papers out of the drawer in a frenzied search for a lost object, to stop them behaving like children who scribble crazily on paper and then ask their parents 'what is it that I've drawn?' The difficulty in philosophizing well is not an intellectual one: it is the difficulty of a conversion. To avoid philosophical nonsense is as hard as it may be to hold back tears or to control one's anger.

By 'phenomenology' Wittgenstein means the attempt to describe the immediately given: under this rubric he discusses the properties of visual space, or rather, the grammar of the description of what is seen. He discusses the problem of colour incompatibility in a way which is familiar since the 'Remarks on Logical Form' of 1929. The chapter on 'Idealism' contains a sustained criticism of the philosophical notion of sense-datum: much of the chapter is very close to the fifth chapter of the *Philosophische Bemerkungen* published in 1964.

The decision whether to publish the Big Typescript as it stood must have been a difficult one for Wittgenstein's literary executors. They appear to have decided against publication principally on the grounds that Wittgenstein was very clearly dissatisfied with what he had written and immediately began to revise it. The first eight chapters and the eleventh chapter of the typescript are covered with manuscript alterations, deletions, additions, revisions, questionings and reorderings. These revisions to the typescript were carried further in the manuscript notebooks. The executors' decision was, in von Wright's words, to publish the new manuscript version of the first two-thirds of text, and the concluding third part of the typescript.

This decision, it seems to me, can be questioned on several grounds. The Big Typescript represents a single, reasonably coherent, stage of Wittgenstein's development: the *Philosophical Grammar* as published does not: the first half of it is a year or more later than the second part, and this at a period when Wittgenstein's thought was evolving fast. If it is said that Wittgenstein would never have published the typescript as it stood, it is equally true that he would never have published the manuscript revision as it stood; in each case, he could have published, but did not. Moreover, there is no reason to believe that Wittgenstein was more satisfied with the later part of the typescript (dealing with philosophy of mathematics) than he was with the earlier part of the typescript (dealing with philosophy of language and mind). The fact that it is not scribbled over, as the first part is, may merely reflect the fact that a point came when Wittgenstein despaired of the whole project of revising the typescript. After all, to the extent that the papers which later became the *Philosophical Investigations* reflect a fresh start in the attempt to discuss the topics of the first part of the typescript, so do the papers which later became the *Remarks on the Foundations of Mathematics* represent a fresh start on the topics of the second part.

In any case, it cannot be said that the published version of the *Philosophical Grammar* results from any systematic application of the criterion that only those parts of the typescript which were not scribbled over should be published. The chapters on philosophy, phenomenology, and idealism present as clean a text to the reader as those on logic and the foundations of mathematics. It cannot be said that they could not be published because they contain passages which duplicate material already published in *Philosophical Investigations* and *Philosophische Bemerkungen*, because that is equally true of many sections which *were* published in the *Philosophical Grammar*. Any reader of the Big Typescript cannot help but find it strange that the omission of these important and fascinating chapters from the published *Grammar* is not only not justified in the editorial note, but not even mentioned there.

Publishing a manuscript revision of the first half of the typescript rather than the original may be defended on the grounds that the revision is a philosophically superior work. Certainly, it is the fruit of maturer philosophical reflection by Wittgenstein, but carried further this defence would lead to the conclusion that once the *Philosophical Investigations* had been published there was little point in publishing the *Grammar* at all. In fact the original Big Typescript contains much of philosophical interest that is not in the revision printed in the Grammar, and much that is in the *Grammar* becomes more intelligible when seen in its earlier and fuller context.

On the other hand, there is also valuable material in the manuscript revisions which is not in the original typescript, and one would applaud an editorial decision that this material should be included (say in a substantial appendix, as the First Quarto text of Hamlet is sometimes printed in editions of Shakespeare as an appendix to the familiar First Folio text) *as well as* the original typescript. But the decision to print *only* a manuscript revision becomes harder to understand once one realizes that it is in fact tendentious to speak as if there *were* a manuscript which could be called '*the* final revision of the Big Typescript'. In fact, it seems to me that one cannot say without artificiality that there came a moment when Wittgenstein *stopped* revising the Big Typescript and *started* writing the *Philosophical Investigations*. The one grew into the other, and the choice of a particular set of manuscripts as the final revision of the typescript is bound to be arbitrary.

To show this, it is necessary to follow in some detail the history of Wittgenstein's revisions. After working over the first part of the typescript, Wittgenstein began a new revision in the middle of manuscript volume X. He did not date this revision – it bears only the notice 'Umarbeitung' – but from its position in the notebook it seems likely that he wrote it in 1933 and the first weeks of 1934. It covered most of the first half of the typescript. It is not written out in order on consecutive pages of the manuscript notebooks; in larger and smaller fragments it covers the second half of volume X and the first half of volume XI. If one starts to read at the beginning, in the middle of volume X, instructions, annotations, arrows, caret marks and cross-references provide an Ariadne's thread which enable one to read a consecutive text in the order Wittgenstein then intended. Later he began a second revision of the first part of the text (sections 1–13 and 23–43 of the published *Grammar*). This 'Zweite Umarbeitung' is written on large separate sheets (the 'Grosses Format' which is no. 140 in von Wright's catalogue). It is this stage of revision – dated by Rhees late 1933 or early 1934 – which is printed in the published *Grammar*.

Once the decision had been taken that it was *this* stage of Wittgenstein's revision that was to be given to the public, the editor's task was to follow the instructions in the manuscripts which passages were to be included and which omitted, and in what order the paragraphs were to occur. this was by no means a trivial or easy task. To give some idea of its magnitude, I will describe what a reader would encounter who opened manuscript volume X at the page in the middle which Wittgenstein numbered '1' when he began his revision or *Umarbeitung*.

Beside the word 'Umbarbeitung' we read 'Zweite Umarbeitung im Grossen Format'. We turn therefore to the beginning of the *Grosses Format* and read its first thirteen pages. These, read consecutively, with the insertion of a number of passages from later pages of the *Grosses Format* which Wittgenstein's caret marks clearly indicate to be inserted, give us the text of pp. 39–50 of the *Philosophical Grammar*. After the words 'multiplizieren können' which end section 12 of the *Grammar* we are instructed by Wittgenstein to insert the paragraphs 'Wie, wenn man fragte . . . auf einmal erleben' from page 14 of the *Grosses Format*. At the end of those paragraphs there appears an instruction in red pencil to continue on p. 28 of volume X. If we turn to that page, we find the material beginning 'Kann ich das. . .' which commences the second chapter of the *Grammar*. To obey the instruction as it stands would have involved omitting the material from pp. 13–14 of the *Grosses Format* which appears on pp. 50–1 of the *Grammatik*; the editor decided, correctly in my opinion, that Wittgenstein had misplaced the instruction and printed the material ('um uns über . . . fragen kann; "welcher!"') as the end of the first chapter.

The passage beginning on p. 28 of volume X is headed, reassuringly 'Fortsetzung von S. 14 Grosses Format'. We read on up to page 33 without difficulty apart from occasional local switches of ordering, crossings-out and decipherment problems. On p. 33 we are instructed to incorporate a passage from p. 93 of the same volume ('Die grammatischen Möglichkeiten . . . ein Signal', *PG* p. 55) and a passage from p. 26 of the *Grosses Format* ('Gefrage . . . etc', *PG*, p. 55). Having done that, we return to p. 33 and read on without difficulty until p. 37 where we are told to incorporate a paragraph from p. 179 of volume X ('Man könnte . . . Sache dar', *PG* p. 57, surprisingly not as a separate paragraph). We then return to p. 37 and are told that the next paragraph is to be replaced by the corresponding one from the typescript. Having done so we are ready for the next instruction to incorporate the passage, 'Wie Augustinus . . . herleitet' (*PG*, p. 57) from p. 179 of volume X. Two pages of comparatively smooth reading are followed by the instruction to include a paragraph from p. 26 of the *Grosses Format* ('Das "nicht" . . . Geste', *PG*, p. 58), and then after a further page from volume X we are told to turn for the continuation to p. 15 of the *Grosses Format*.

It would be tedious to narrate in similar detail the story of how we stay with the *Grosses Format* until its thirty-eighth page, leap to pp. 180–4 of volume X, then back for the last couple of pages of the *Grosses Format*, then take up the thread at p. 59 of volume X, and follow it back and forth through the remainder of that volume, with occasional excursions into the first part of volume XI until we reach the section about a language composed entirely of commands which occurs on p. 179 of volume X and is printed at the end of Part One of the *Grammar*. Enough has been said to show both the task facing the editor in reconstructing the text, and the difficulty there would have been in recording in annotations the editorial decisions taken. With the best will in the world it is very difficult to describe the actual state of the MS in a way which makes clear to someone who does not have both the MSS and the printed *Grammar* in front of him which decisions were Wittgenstein's and which were the editor's.

None the less, Wittgenstein's instructions are not always un-ambiguous, and though in general his intentions seem to have been teased out and carried out with remarkable fidelity by the editor, it seems to me that in several places they have been ignored or misunderstood, in one place with the effect that three paragraphs (the paragraphs 'Wenn ich . . .' 'Wenn man . . .' 'Wenn ich . . .' on p. 75 of volume X) have been omitted against Wittgenstein's instructions. No doubt no two editors would have reached the same decisions about this difficult text. In order to enable readers of the *Grammar* to see for themselves the nature of the problems involved and the decisions to be taken, I now give a (slightly schematic) list of the immediate sources of the printed *Philosophical Grammar*, which enable its text to be compared with the MSS and typescripts in Trinity College Cambridge.

Philo-sophical Grammar	Source	VW catalogue numbers & pages
Part One		
§§ 1–13	*Grosses Format (Zweite Umarbeitung)*	140, 1–14 etc.
§§ 14–22	Volume X (*Umarbeitung*)	114, 45–51 etc.
§§ 23–40	*Grosses Format (Zweite Umarbeitung)*	140, 15–39
§§ 41–2	Volume X (*Umarbeitung*)	114, 121–2
§ 42 ('Wie verhalt. . .)	*Grosses Format*	140, 38
§§ 43–95	Volume X	114, 59–102 etc.
§§ 96–107	Volume X	114, 132–44
§§108–14	Volume X	114, 103–8 etc.
§§115–31	Volume XI	115, 1–31
§§132–41	Volume X	114, 108–18 etc.
Appendices		
1–3	*Three Essays*	214, 1–15
4a	Big Typescript, sec. 28	213, 100–1
4b	Volume XII	116, 80
5–8	Big Typescript, secs. 31–4	213, 113–42

---

[1] Page numbers given here are actual folio numbers of the volumes, not (as in the text above) the numbers written on them by Wittgenstein.

Part Two

One of the most important tasks for the editor of the manuscript revision was to decide where it came to an end. There is no immediately obvious reason for the point in fact chosen by the editor. As can be seen from the above chart the revision, having penetrated well into volume XI, then returns for a number of pages into volume X. The last pages of consecutive text in volume X include a forward reference to volume XI, from which the steam-roller passage (*PG*, p. 194) is taken. We then return back from the command-language passage which ends part one of the *Grammar*. It is followed, in the last pages of volume X, by passages which have been earmarked for inclusion earlier, as have the first pages of volume XI. If we go on – following the procedure often adopted in volume X – to find the continuation of the main text in the next passage not earmarked for backspacing, we come to p. 37 of volume XI. The long continuous passage which begins there could very well be regarded as a consecutive passage of a revision of the Big Typescript: it includes, for instance, a version of a passage about Moses from chapter seven of the typescript (which is, of course, familiar to readers of the *Investigations*). It is a pity that the editorial note to the *Grammar* does not give reasons for the choice of stopping point.

The reader will have gathered that a number of passages in the *Philosophical Grammar* appeared in four different recensions during the period whose history we have been following: first, in the Big Typescript, then in the interlinear corrections in the Big Typescript, then in the *Umarbeitung* in volume X, then in the *Zweite Umarbeitung* in the *Grosses Format*. But the greatest complication of the story is yet to be told. No. 116 in von Wright's catalogue is the manuscript notebook XII. It is thus described by him:

In 116 – the largest volume in the series – three parts can be distinguished. The first (pp. 1–265) is best described as another effort of Wittgenstein's to compose a book, stating his position. (Within this first part of 116 one can distinguish two subparts of roughly equal length, the second beginning on page 135.) It begins as a revision of material in the early portions of 213 (The Big Typescript), but becomes more and more unlike 213, moving, so to speak, in the direction of the *Investigations*. The second part of 116 (pp. 265–315) has the character of revisions of writings in the earlier volumes and contains much that is included in the *Investigations*. The third part (pp. 316–347) is to some extent a revision of the content of the second part and likewise closely related to the *Investigations*.

The manuscript volume 116 was bought in Bergen, Norway. This is a strong indication that the earliest entries in the volume cannot have been made before some time in the summer of 1936. It is a plausible conjecture that the whole of the first part of the volume was written in 1936, and before the end of August. . . .

Volume XII is extremely difficult to fit into the history of the revision of the Big Typescript. Both von Wright and Rhees believe that it is substantially later than the *Zweite Umarbeitung* (cf. *PG*, p. 211). The reader who approaches volume XII in this belief is astonished to find that the revision it contains is, at least at the beginning, very much closer to the original text of the Big Typescript than are either of the earlier revisions. This fact alone, if the accepted chronology is correct, surely casts doubt on any claim of the *Zweite Umarbeitung* to be *the* final revision of the typescript: it means that *after* the second revision Wittgenstein came to the conclusion that his book would do better to stick closer to the original text of the typescript.

On the other hand, one may wonder whether the dating of the *Grosses Format* by von Wright and Rhees in 1933–4 is correct. May it be that the *Grosses Format* is *later* than the Volume XII revision? There are some slight indications of this; the placing of the passage about chess after the passage about Frege against the formalists (*PG*, p. 40) appears as an afterthought in volume XII and is written fair in the *Grosses Format*; on the verso of the last page of the *Grosses Format* appears the first paragraph of the *Philosophical Investigations*, of which the first version is dated by von Wright in September or later of 1936. If this were so, then the chronological and developmental gap between the first and the second half of the printed version of the *Philosophical Grammar* would be even larger than at first appeared.

I am not competent to settle this difficult question about the chronology of Wittgenstein's manuscripts. But however it is resolved, the existence of volume XII must surely support the contention that the most prudent editorial policy would have been to print the original Big Typescript as it stood rather than to seek for a definitive revision of it.

In 1971 von Wright and a number of other scholars printed a handsome and scholarly edition of Wittgenstein's early *Prototractatus*. The scale of this edition shows the difficulty and expense of reproducing on the printed page the meticulous and thoroughgoing revision to which Wittgenstein subjected his writing. The Big Typescript is much longer than, and underwent much more drastic revision than, the *Prototractatus*. An edition of it in the style of the *Prototractatus* edition would no doubt involve expense far in excess of any foreseeable gain to philosophical scholarship. But we must hope that in some form or other Wittgenstein's literary executors will offer to the public those substantial portions of the typescript which are inadequately represented by the published *Philosophical Grammar*.

4

Wittgenstein on the Nature
of Philosophy

One of the most constant features of Wittgenstein's philosophy throughout his life, was his view of the nature of philosophy itself. In this paper I shall discuss his view of philosophy in the central period of his life, the period which began with his return to the subject of philosophy in the late 1920s. In the early thirties Wittgenstein began work on a book which at one time he gave a substantial form as what is known as the Big Typescript – a 700-page typescript divided into chapters and headed paragraphs. He was immediately dissatisfied with it; it was never meant for publication but only as a basis for publication, and he continually revised it. One of the revisions of it, edited by Rush Rhees, has been published under the title *Philosophical Grammar*. Wittgenstein continued to work at perfecting the form and content of his philosophical ideas until he died, leaving a version of his thoughts which he regarded as publishable and which is known to us as *Philosophical Investigations*. I shall concentrate on the period of Wittgenstein's life between those two books and shall be drawing on unpublished parts very largely: I shall quote some familiar passages from *Philosophical Investigations* but I shall also draw partly on the Big Typescript (whose sections on philosophy do not appear in *Philosophical Grammar*) and partly on other unpublished manuscripts of the thirties.[1]

The problem from which I start is this. Wittgenstein seems at first sight to have two rather different views of philosophy. On the

---

[1] I shall refer to MSS by the numbers in von Wright's 'The Wittgenstein Papers', *Philosophical Review*, 79 (1969), pp. 483–503.

one hand, he often compares philosophy to a medical technique, to a therapy, a method of healing. On the other, he seems to see philosophy as giving overall understanding, a clear view of the world.

In a familiar sentence of *Philosophical Investigations* Wittgenstein says: 'The philosopher's treatment of a question is like the treatment of an illness' (*PI*, I §255). Philosophy is not a single therapy, but a set of therapies: 'There is not *a* philosophical method, though there are indeed methods, like different therapies' (*PI*, I, §133). When one hears philosophy compared to a therapy, one thinks principally of psychotherapy, but Wittgenstein also thought of philosophy as being like physical medicine, as like a cure for physical diseases. He said – again I quote a familiar passage of *Philosophical Investigations*, but one written in the early thirties – 'The results of philosophy are the uncovering of one or another piece of plain nonsense and of bumps that the understanding has got by running its head up against the limits of language. These bumps make us see the value of the discovery' (*PI*, I, §119, MS 213, 425). but philosophy is a medicine which is sometimes curative and sometimes preventive: a way in which it is preventive is suggested by a remark in English in his notebooks. 'Philosophical questions, when you boil them down to what they really amount to, change their aspect entirely. What evaporates is what the intellect cannot take.' (MS 159, 3b) The metaphor of boiling down is meant seriously: we are to think of a dietitian who has to cater to an invalid with a weak stomach, which cannot take certain foods. So the philosopher (the true philosopher) will boil down the philosophical problems so that our intellects can take them.

It is especially to psychoanalysis – and to psychotherapy in general – that Wittgenstein compares his philosophy. Wittgenstein was impressed by, and critical of, the work of Freud: he thought that his own method was a method of analysis. The comparison is made explicitly in a passage from *Philosophical Grammar*, with particular reference to the philosophy of mathematics. Wittgenstein is saying that mathematicians are very unhappy when they read what he writes on the philosophy of mathematics. They think that what he has to say is too simple, that he discusses difficulties that only a child would take seriously. Then Wittgenstein says this:

A mathematician is bound to be horrified by my mathematical comments, since he has always been trained to avoid indulging in thoughts and doubts of the kind I develop. He has learned to regard them as something contemptible and, to use an analogy from psychoanalysis (this paragraph is reminiscent of Freud), he has acquired a revulsion from them as infantile. That is to say, I trot out all the problems that a child learning arithmetic, etc., finds difficult, the problems that education represses without solving. I say to those repressed doubts: you are quite correct, go on asking, demand clarification! (*PG*, pp. 381–2)

So, one thing that philosophical therapy involves for mathematicians, is giving expression to repressed doubts, repressed puzzlements, things that one was told not to take any notice of – 'Learn mathematics, and then you won't worry any more about these doubts'. This connects with a well-known saying of Wittgenstein that one of the things he wanted to do in philosophy was to turn *latent* nonsense into *patent* nonsense. When we are suffering from philosophical problems we have a bit of hidden nonsense in our minds, and the only way to cure it is to bring it out into the open. Very often, for instance, he attacks a mythology which we have about the nature of the mind. We imagine a mechanism in the mind, some strange mechanism which is capable of working very well in its own mysterious medium but which if understood as a mechanism in the ordinary sense is totally unintelligible. Wittgenstein thinks this is a bit of latent or hidden nonsense. The way to make it explicit is to imagine that mechanism really existed. You may think, for instance, that when you recognize somebody, what you do is to consult a sort of mental picture of him and check whether what you now see matches this picture. Wittgenstein suggests that if we have this nonsense picture in our mind we can make ourselves see that it is nonsense, that it in no way explains recognition. If we imagine it as happening in the real world and suppose that the picture is a real picture, on a piece of paper, the problem just returns: how do I recognize that this is a picture of a particular person in order to use it to recognize him? So this is a form of psychoanalytic therapy, in that something which is a *repressed* bit of nonsense in my mind is then made *explicit* nonsense. I give expression to it, just as in a Freudian treatment I make explicit my repressed emotions: this is part of the way of being cured of the bad results of the repression.

Another way in which the philosophical method of Wittgenstein resembles that of psychoanalysis is that in certain areas what the patient says goes, that is, the patient's acceptance of an interpretation has a specially crucial role. The patient for analysis in philosophy, of course, is the person who is suffering from a philosophical error. In philosophy in general, Wittgenstein says, there is usually no question of finding a precise description of phenomena, but if you are describing a philosophical error, you must describe it absolutely accurately; that is, the person who is under the influence of the error must say: 'Yes, that's what I think, that's exactly what I think.' He says: 'We can bring someone's mistake home to him only when he acknowledges it as the right expression for what he feels. . . . The point is: only when he acknowledges it as such *is* it the right expression' – and then in brackets: '(Psychoanalysis)' (MS 213, 410).

The analogy between philosophy and psychoanalysis is an important and fruitful one. But rather than to develop it further, I want to ask a particular question about it. If philosophy is therapeutic – whether in a physical sense or in the psychoanalytic sense – then must not the role of philosophy be a negative one? Philosophy, it seems, is only useful to people who are sick in some way; a healthy person – a person of healthy mind and healthy body – has no need of philosophy.

This seems very different from the view of philosophy as building great systems, the traditional view of philosophy. Wittgenstein certainly agrees that philosophy has a destructive role, though he also says that what it destroys is not worth preserving. There is a well-known passage in *Philosophical Investigations*:

> Where does our investigation get its importance from, since it seems only to destroy everything interesting, that is, all that is great and important? (As it were all the buildings, leaving behind only bits of stone and rubble.) What we are destroying is nothing but houses of cards, and we are clearing up the ground of language on which they stand. (*PI*, I, §118)

There is an earlier, perhaps even more vivid, expression of the same idea that philosophy is a destroyer in the Big Typescript: "All that philosophy can do is to destroy idols. And that means not making any new ones – say out of 'the absence of idols'" (MS 213, 413).

So philosophy is a destroyer of idols and of castles in the air. This view of philosophy seems to be a very negative view of philosophy, in which philosophy has only a critical role. But on the other hand, one can also find in Wittgenstein's writings evidence of what seems at first a different and more positive view of philosophy, a view of philosophy as giving a special kind of understanding, of giving a very general view of the world, an overall understanding. For instance, he says in a passage which occurs over and over again between the 1930s and the 1940s: 'A main source of our failure to understand is that we do not *command a clear view* of the use of our words. Our grammar is lacking in perspicuity. . . . The concept of a perspicuous representation is of fundamental significance for us. It earmarks the form of account we give, the way we look at things' (*PI*, I, §122). And then he asks: 'Is this a Weltanschauung?' and in earlier versions, in place of that question, he had said: 'A sort of Weltanschauung that seems to be typical of our times. Spengler' (*MS* 213, 417). An early metaphor for this idea that philosophy gives us an overall view – an *Übersicht* – and how it does it, appears in a passage from the Big Typescript:

> A philosophical question is like an inquiry into the constitution of society. It is as if a society met without clear written rules but in a situation where rules are necessary: the members have an instinct that enables them to observe certain rules in their dealings with one another, but everything is made more difficult because there is no clear pronouncement on the subject, no arrangement for clarifying the rules. Thus they regard one of their number as president, but he does not sit at the head of the table nor is he in any way recognizable and this makes the transaction of business more difficult. So we come along and bring order and clarity. We seat the president at an easily identifiable place with his secretary near him at a special little table, and we seat the other, ordinary members in two rows on either side of the table and so on. . . . (MS 213, 415)

This suggests a certain re-ordering of things by the philosopher, to make everything clear. Not everything in this quotation from the

Big Typescript would fit, I think, his view later. But even in *Philosophical Investigations* he says this: 'We want to establish an order in our knowledge of the use of language: an order with a particular end in view; one out of many possible orders – not *the* order . . . . the clarity that we are aiming at is indeed *complete* clarity' (*PI*, I, §§132–3). So, it is the task of philosophy to achieve an order, an order which gives complete clarity. This seems much more like some of the traditional, almost imperialistic, views of philosophy than the mere therapeutic view of philosophy as preventing you from banging your head against the limits of language. Wittgenstein is even ready to call philosophy a search for essences: 'if we . . . in these investigations are trying to understand the essence of language . . . this means something that already lies open to view and that becomes surveyable by a rearrangement' (*PI*, I, §92). Though this view of philosophy as looking for an order which makes everything surveyable is in some ways like the traditional view of philosophy, Wittgenstein insists that previous philosophy, and especially his own previous philosophy – in *Tractatus Logico-Philosophicus* – went about its search for *Wesen*, for essence, in the wrong way. He makes a contrast between looking at things as a whole to obtain an overview, and trying to penetrate things to see their metaphysical works, to see what makes them tick, from a metaphysical point of view. He says, describing this mistaken view: 'We feel as if we had to *penetrate* phenomena' (*PI*, I, §90), 'The *essence is hidden from us*' (*PI*, I, §92); 'Something that lies within, which we see when we look *into* the thing, and which an analysis digs out' (*PI*, I, §92).

In particular, Wittgenstein thought, in his earlier philosophy, he had falsely tried to generalize genuine insights. For instance, he had thought that a proposition was a picture. This was the genuine insight, but he had mistakenly tried to make *all* propositions of any kind also be pictures. If they did not look like pictures, this must be because we could not see through them; if we could see sufficiently deep inside they really are pictures. That was his view in the *Tractatus*, which now he rejects. He says: 'The fatal thing about the scientific way of thinking, which the whole world employs nowadays, is that it wants to produce an explanation in answer to each anxiety.'

Of the *Tractatus* he says:

> I had used a simile, but because of the grammatical illusion that a concept word has a single thing corresponding to it, the common element in all the objects it applies to, the simile did not seem like one.
>
> Now we have a *theory* . . . but it does not look like a theory. It is typical of such a theory to look at a particular case which is in clear view and say '*That* shows how matters stand in general: this case is the paradigm of every case.' 'Of course' we say 'that's how it has to be' and we have a feeling of satisfaction. We have reached a form of representation which appears *self-evident* to us. But it seems as if we have had a vision of something lying *beneath* the surface. This tendency to generalize the clear case seems to be strictly justified in logic: here we seem to be fully justified in concluding: 'If *one* proposition is a picture, then every proposition must be a picture, because they must all share a common essence.' For we do indeed suffer from the illusion that the sublime and essential part of our investigation resides in grasping a single all-embracing essence.

That quotation is from the early version of *Philosophical Investigations* which was written before the war (MS 220, 92). It does not appear in the final version of *Philosophical Investigations*. But it is interesting to note his reaction to the picture theory of the *Tractatus* even at this late date. He does not, in effect, say: 'It was a total mistake; I was quite wrong to think a proposition was like a picture'. He says: 'Yes, yes, there is a very clear case in which a proposition is very much like a picture; I was wrong to think that *all* propositions were like this.'

Wittgenstein objects to traditional philosophy that it claims to *explain* things, to discover new truths. As early as 1913, in his very earliest surviving work on philosophy, he said that philosophy must only describe, it cannot explain, it must not try to explain. So that it was no new thought in the 1930s that philosophy was not a scientific explanation. But Wittgenstein did come to think that his own *Tractatus* had fallen into the error that it was designed to avoid, that is, of treating philosophy as if it were a kind of science. I quote from *Philosophical Investigations* a passage where he is discussing this *Tractatus* view.

It was true to say that our considerations could not be scientific ones. . . . We may not advance any kind of theory. There must not be anything hypothetical in our considerations. We must do away with all *explanation*, and description alone must take its place. And this description gets its light, that is to say its purpose, from the philosophical problems. These are, of course, not empirical problems; they are solved, rather, by looking into the workings of our language, and that in such a way as to make us recognize those workings: in despite of an urge to misunderstand them. The problems are solved, not by giving new information, but by arranging what we have always known. (*PI*, I, §109)

One feature of all this is important to emphasize in order to reconcile the overview theory of philosophy with the therapeutic theory of philosophy. That is, that Wittgenstein insists that philosophy is only philosophical problems. The survey which you make does not give you the kind of totally new understanding, a surplus understanding, it merely removes the philosophical problems. Philosophy is not anything over and above the problems and their removal. The clearest statements of this are in *Philosophical Grammar*, but they are echoed later. Wittgenstein says in *Philosophical Grammar*:

Philosophy isn't anything except philosophical problems, the particular individual worries that we call 'philosophical problems'. Their common element extends as far as the common element in different regions of our language. (*PG*, p. 193)

'Philosophy', like so many other words, is a family-likeness word: there is no one thing in common to everything that is philosophy. In the same context, having said that '*Sprache*' – language – is a family-likeness concept, so that there is no single essence of language, he goes on to say:

If the general concept of language dissolves in this way, doesn't philosophy dissolve as well? No, for the task of philosophy is not to create a new, ideal language, but to clarify the use of our language . . . . its aim is to remove particular misunderstandings; not to produce a real understanding for the first time. (*PG*, p. 115)

There is one philosophical remark to which Wittgenstein attached great importance: he wrote it very early on, it is in the Big Typescript and earlier, and it appears also in *Philosophical Investigations*, but he continued to reconsider it after *Philosophical Investigations* was all ready for the press. It is the following remark:

> The real discovery is the one that makes me capable of stopping doing philosophy when I want to – the one that gives philosophy peace, so that it is no longer tormented by questions which bring *itself* in question. – Instead, we now demonstrate a method, by examples; and the series of examples can be broken off. – Problems are solved (difficulties eliminated), not a *single* problem. . . . 'But then we will never come to the end of our job!' Of course not, because it has no end. (MS, 213, 431f)

Now, why did Wittgenstein say that the important discovery was the one that let him stop doing philosophy whenever he wanted? It seems a very strange thing to say. It would be absurd to say, for instance, that the most important musical discovery is the one which enables you to stop making music when you want. Why should he say the important discovery in philosophy is one that enables you to stop philosophizing?

What Wittgenstein is attacking there is the view that philosophy is something that you have to do before you can do anything else; the view that until philosophy has been gotten over with nothing else is reliable; the view that philosophy is a *foundation* of things. Such a view was held very explicitly by Descartes. Descartes said that knowledge was a tree of which metaphysics – by which he meant largely epistemology – was the root, with physics as the trunk and various branches such as medicine, mechanics, and morals. What Wittgenstein is attacking is the idea that the whole tree will not grow unless you have the roots, the metaphor implicit in the description of philosophical studies as being foundational studies. Clearly, if you have the foundational view of philosophy you cannot stop philosophizing whenever you want to; until you get these roots dug in, until you get the foundations built, you cannot do anything else, so it would be irresponsible for the philosopher to stop. The real discovery, then, is the one that you can stop when you want to – you are not going to spoil anything else.

There are many passages in Wittgenstein which attack the idea that philosophy provides a foundation. For instance:

> Philosophy solves, or rather gets rid of, only philosophical problems; it does not set our thinking on a more solid basis. What I am attacking is above all the idea that the question 'what is knowledge' – e.g. – is a crucial one. That is what it seems to be: it seems as if we didn't yet know anything at all until we can answer *that* question. In our philosophical investigations it is as if we were in a terrible hurry to complete a backlog of unfinished business which has to be finished or else everything else seems to hang in the air. (MS 219, 10)

In fact it is quite absurd to say: 'We cannot know anything at all until we know what knowing is.' To use an example Wittgenstein often uses, that is as foolish as to say: 'We cannot spell any words at all, unless we can spell "spelling".' There is no metamathematics, Wittgenstein says, philosophy is not meta-anything; that is, it is not a science which studies a discipline as a whole and gives it a foundation. It is not a second-order activity at all. 'One might think: if philosophy speaks of the use of the word "philosophy" there must be a second-order philosophy' (*PI*, I, §121). 'The philosophy of logic speaks of sentences and words in exactly the same sense in which we speak of them in ordinary life . . .' (*PI*, I, §108). Orthography is not a second-order science: you spell the word 'spelling' the same way as you spell any other word.

Now I come to my main question. If the value of philosophy is simply that it gets rid of philosophical worries, and that it solves philosophical problems, then why do philosophy at all? Is there not a simpler way of getting rid of these worries and these problems, namely, never look at a book of philosophy! Do not get as far as the problems and then you will not need the answers! Thus you would be saved a lot of anguish and society would be saved a lot of money. If philosophy is only good against philosophers, why do philosophy at all?

At best, philosophy might be like germ warfare. Several countries have establishments for inventing the most terrible weapons of germ warfare. If you meet people who work in these establishments you naturally wonder at them and ask: 'Why do you work at this kind of job – inventing new diseases to give to human beings?' They always give you the answer: 'We need to know what it may be that our enemies are planning. Unless we try and invent things for use against others we will not know what terrible things *they* are going to do to us. We do not really intend to give these diseases to everybody else, we just want to know how to deal with them if other people use such weapons against us.' On this account of Wittgenstein's view of philosophy it seems as if philosophers are people like those who work in a germ warfare department. It is perhaps justifiable to work on these strange cultures that are going to produce the most extraordinary intellectual diseases, but it is justifiable only on the count that there are already other people who are producing these horrible things and you have to produce them yourself to know how to deal with them.

Not liking the comparison between philosophy and germ warfare I want to look at what Wittgenstein says to see if there is perhaps another way that one can interpret it. 'What is the use of philosophy if it is only useful against other philosophers?' is a question that was put with characteristic vigour by Professor Gilbert Ryle. You remember one of Wittgenstein's most famous descriptions of the purpose of philosophy is given in *Philosophical Investigations*: 'What is your aim in philosophy? – To show the fly the way out of the fly-bottle' (*PI*, I, §309). Ryle asked: 'What has a fly lost, who never got into a fly-bottle?'

In an unpublished manuscript there is a very clear answer to the question 'Why do philosophy, if it is only useful against philosophers?' Wittgenstein says: 'Philosophy is a tool which is useful only against philosophers and against the philosopher in us' (MS 219, 11). It is only useful against philosophers, yes, but also against *the philosopher in us*. Wittgenstein's answer to the question 'Why do philosophy at all, if it is only useful against philosophical errors?' is that every one of us, every human being, is trapped in philosophical errors. And there are a number of indications that suggest Wittgenstein believed philosophy to be an unavoidable part of the human condition. He quotes with approval, for instance, the remark of Lichtenberg: 'Our whole philosophy is the rectification of linguistic usage: the rectification, that is, of a philosophy which is the most universal philosophy.' I think Wittgenstein endorsed the idea. In the Big Typescript he says: 'Philosophy is embodied not in propositions, but in a language' (MS 213, 425). The philosophy which is embedded in our language is a bad philosophy – it is a mythology. Wittgenstein says. 'In our language there is an entire mythology embodied' (MS 213, 434). He gives an instance of what he means: 'The primitive forms of our language – noun, adjective, and verb – show the simple picture to which it tries to make everything conform.'

When Wittgenstein says that there is a mythology in our language, this is not a total condemnation (Wittgenstein's attitude to myths was a many-sided one), but it is not a justification either. Some myths, certainly, are something to be got rid of; and if some are to be retained, we must recognize them as myths. The question then is in what way – according to Wittgenstein – is the philosopher better off than an ordinary non-philosopher? Is there any way in which he is better off? The answer, I think, is yes. This does not mean that it is to everybody's advantage to become a philosopher; but if you do philosophy in the right spirit, then you are better off than somebody who has done no philosophy. It is not because you know more that you are better off: you do not know anything that anybody else does not know, and one of the temptations of philosophy, which makes it a dangerous thing to take up, is that you may get the impression that you do know more than other people. But still, you are better off, if you have done philosophy in the right way: not because you know more, but because you have gone through a discipline which enables you to resist certain temptations.

This comes out in a remark of Wittgenstein's about Tolstoy. In 'What is Art?' Tolstoy makes it the criterion of value for a work of art that it should be intelligible to everybody; that is why certain short stories and the Bible are magnificent art but why the operas of the nineteenth-century composers are totally worthless. I quote from the Big Typescript:

> Tolstoy: 'The significance of an object lies in its universal intelligibility'. That is partly true, partly false. When an object is significant and important what makes it difficult to understand is not the lack of some special instruction in abstruse matters necessary for its

understanding, but the conflict between the right understanding of the object and what most men *want* to see. This can make the most obvious things the most difficult to understand. What has to be overcome is not a difficulty of the understanding, but of the will. (MS 213, 406–7)

And he says that in philosophy as in architecture: 'The job to be done is . . . really a job on oneself' (*ibid.*).

Wittgenstein thinks that the task of philosophy is not to enlighten the intellect, or not directly, but to work upon the will, to strengthen one to resist certain temptations. Wittgenstein's account of why we have to philosophize, or why it is worthwhile to philosophize even though philosophy is only useful against philosophical problems, is rather like the Christian doctrine of original sin. According to the Christian doctrine we are all born in a state of sin; according to Wittgenstein we are not born in the state of philosophical sin, but we take it in along with language. Along with language, along with all the benefits which language brings, along with all the possibilities for our way of life which it brings, we take in whether we want to or not, certain temptations; we must resist these if we are not to be misled. There are several passages where Wittgenstein speaks of the temptation or bewitchment of language. One very well-known one from *Philosophical Investigations* concerns the philosophy of mathematics and the inclination we have to say certain things about mathematics.

> What we 'are tempted to say' in such a case, is, of course, not philosophy – but its raw material. Thus, for example, what a mathematician is inclined to say about the objectivity and reality of mathematical facts, is not a philosophy of mathematics, but something for philosophical *treatment*. (*PI*, I, §254)

In the Big Typescript Wittgenstein gives a lively illustration of the temptations. He says:

> Learning philosophy has the same kind of extraordinary difficulty that geography lessons would have if the pupils began with a lot of false and oversimplified ideas about the way rivers and mountain ranges go. (MS 213, 423)

It is as with the maps which the railways, for example the London Underground, provide, which simplify the way in which the railways go; they make it look as if they go in rectangular tracks. Wittgenstein is suggesting that we come to learn the philosophy of language with a sort of preconception as if a child coming to a geography lesson believed that the railway maps showed the shape in which the world was, that the rivers and mountains were all square, etc.

> Human beings are profoundly enmeshed in philosophical – i.e. grammatical – confusions. They cannot be freed without first being extricated from the extraordinary variety of associations which hold them prisoner. You have as it were to reconstitute their entire language. – But this language grew up as it did because human beings had – and have – the tendency to think in this way. So you can only succeed in extricating people who live in an instinctive rebellion against language; you cannot help those whose entire instinct is to live in the herd which has created this language as its own proper mode of expression. (MS 213, 423)

This, to my ear, resembles the type of language of St Augustine. Augustine thought that we were all a '*massa damnata*': by being born into this race we were born into a damned race, and only those who were not at home in the world, those who found that they had to push against it, really had a hope of salvation. The comparison between philosophy and conversion, philosophy and renunciation of the world, is very explicit in the Big Typescript. Just as Augustine would think that in renouncing the world, the flesh, and the devil one is not giving up anything that is really worthwhile, so Wittgenstein says about philosophy:

> As I have often said, philosophy does not call on me for any sacrifice, because I am not denying myself the saying of anything but simply giving up certain combinations of words as senseless. But in another sense philosophy demands a renunciation, but a renunciation of feeling, not of understanding. Perhaps that is what makes it so hard for many people. It can be as hard to refrain from using an expression as it is to hold back tears or hold in anger. (MS 213, 406)

Up to this point then, the answer to the question 'Why go into philosophy?' is that we are all philosophers, bad or good, whether we choose it or not; we are made philosophers by our language. But that is not the full answer to the question, because Wittgenstein also often says that philosophical errors or problems do not trouble us in practical life. The title of a whole section of the Big Typescript goes like this:

> It is not in practical life that we encounter philosophical problems (as we may encounter scientific problems) – it is when we start constructing sentences not for practical purposes but under the influence of certain analogies in language. (MS 213, 427)

And in several places he says that Augustine's question 'What is time?' is not the kind of thing that really bothers people when they are using their watches or keeping appointments.

> Someone who is engaged in measuring time will not be bothered by this problem. He will *use* language and not notice the problem at all. In his hand, we might say, language is soft and pliable; in the hands of others – philosophers – it suddenly becomes hard and stiff and begins to display difficulties. Philosophers as it were freeze language and make it rigid. (MS 219, 24)

It is when language is idling, etc., that these difficulties come. Why then do philosophy if philosophical confusion does no practical harm? I conjecture that Wittgenstein would answer as follows. An ordinary person, a simple human being who takes no interest in philosophy, has as a user of language a temptation to all kinds of philosophical misunderstandings. If he is lucky these will not harm him at all; certainly they will not harm him when he is going about his daily business. However, he is liable to suffer in two ways.

First of all, the plain man is vulnerable to the persuasions of the bad philosophers and the bad scientists. Let us suppose he is a victim of the mythology of the mental process, the belief that all kinds of strange mental processes go on in cases where experience reveals no such process, but our language suggests that one must occur. Such a person is not impeded in his communication with other people in the ordinary way by these theories, but on the other hand, he may come across a psychologist who has built a theory on them and on its basis erected doctrines about how children shall be taught in school. Without philosophy you are defenceless against that sort of pseudoscientific persuasion.

Secondly, not only is the plain man vulnerable in that way, but he is weak in another way. He is unqualified to go in for any scientific inquiry, because once he investigates anything scientifically, the philosophical errors will then begin to matter. In terms of the medical analogy, he is like somebody with a weak heart, who, if he lives a quiet life, and if there are no epidemics, may well live as long and as peaceful a life as everybody else, but because his heart is weak he may be one of the first people who suffer when an epidemic comes in and who will not be good for any expedition which involves climbing mountains or going into difficult climates. The non-philosophical person, if he takes up a science, is like a man with a weak heart who tries to climb Mount Everest; the philosophical errors from ordinary language that have not impeded him in milking his cows or sewing his shirt, begin really to matter.

Even before that, in addition to being vulnerable to pseudoscientists the plain man is vulnerable to bad mythology. Wittgenstein, despite his sympathetic attitude to mythology, thought that there could be very bad mythologies: he felt, for instance, that the doctrine of the scapegoat was a bad mythology. The idea that you could get rid of your guilt and put it on to an animal, understood simply as mythology, is a bad, a degrading, thing to believe. This is an instance of the kind of thing which the plain man without philosophy is vulnerable to. If he then takes a step further and tries to turn his bad mythology into a theology, if he makes it scientific study, then of course it is worse. In the Big Typescript Wittgenstein says that crude ideas of the soul are less dangerous than sophisticated ones:

> As long as you imagine the soul as a *thing*, a *body* in the head, this hypothesis is not at all dangerous. It is not the crudity and incompleteness of our models that brings danger, but their vagueness.

> The danger begins when we notice that the old model is inadequate and then instead of altering it as it were sublimate it. As long as I say

that thought is in my head, there is nothing wrong; things become dangerous when we say that thought is not in my head but in my spirit. (MS 213, 434–5)

There are then, three areas of danger for someone undisciplined by philosophy: at the mythical level, at the hypermythical or theological level, and at the scientific level.

Wittgenstein's views on the relationship between science and philosophy are difficult to understand. On the one hand, he seems to say that philosophy leaves all the other sciences just as they are, has nothing to say to them, does not alter them or give them foundations. At the same time, he seems to say that unless you are a philosopher you are going to make the most terrible scientific mistakes. He says this especially in connection with the two sciences whose philosophy he was most interested in: psychology and mathematics. There is a familiar passage in *Philosophical Investigations*:

> Philosophy may in no way interfere with the actual use of language – it can in the end only describe it.
> For it cannot give it any foundation either.
> It leaves everything as it is.
> It also leaves mathematics as it is, and no mathematical discovery can advance it. (*PI*, I, §124)

It is, I think, misleading to say that philosophy leaves mathematics exactly as it is. In the sense in which Wittgenstein means it, it is correct; but the obvious way to read that passage is that mathematics and philosophy are independent of each other and progress in one cannot affect progress in the other, a mistake in one cannot affect a mistake in the other. That is not what he means, as you only have to set beside this text a rather comic passage about mathematics and philosophy in *Philosophical Grammar* in order to see.

> Philosophical clarity will have the same effect on the growth of mathematics as sunlight has on the growth of potato shoots. (In a dark cellar they grow yards long.) (*PG*, p. 381)

If it is true that mathematics will grow to a gigantic length if it is left in its dark cellar, but in the daylight of philosophy will only grow so big, then how can we say that philosophy leaves mathematics just as it is? In fact there are numerous passages which show that Wittgenstein thought that philosophy does affect other disciplines in practice, especially mathematics and psychology. For instance he says that it is simple philosophical mistakes that mathematicians make which lead them to make very complicated mistakes in mathematics.

> If a philosopher draws the attention of a mathematician to a distinction, or a misleading mode of expression, the mathematician always says 'Sure, we know all that, it isn't really very interesting.' He does not realize that when he is troubled by philosophical questions it is because of those very unclarities that he passed over earlier with a shrug of the shoulders. (MS 219, 10)

And again from *Philosophical Grammar*:

> A philosopher feels changes in the style of a derivation which a contemporary mathematician passes over calmly with a blank face. What will distinguish the mathematician of the future from those of today will really be a greater sensitivity, and *that* will – as it were – prune mathematics; since people will then be more intent on absolute clarity than on the discovery of new games. (*PG*, p. 381)

The solution to this apparent inconsistency about the relationship between philosophy and mathematics is this: that mathematics as a discipline is not responsible to philosophy; but the people who are mathematicians are human beings who suffer from the original sin of using the philosophically misleading language. It is not while they are doing mathematics but while they are talking ordinary language about mathematics that they reveal their philosophical mistakes. This may, human nature being what it is, lead them also to make mistakes or useless moves in their mathematics.

Wittgenstein says, strikingly, that the philosopher is not a citizen of any human community, and that is what makes him a philosopher. And he contrasts the good philosopher, who stands outside the human communities, with bourgeois philosophers of whom he gives Frank Ramsey as an example. He regarded Ramsey as a bourgeois philosopher because he was willing to take mathematics more or less as it stood and just as the mathematicians of his age described it. According to Wittgenstein he was a sort of propagandist for the current regime in mathematics. The real philosopher must stand outside. Of course, he stands outside mathematics because he is a philosopher and not a mathematician; but Wittgenstein means something more than that: he must distance himself from the mathematical community, that is, the community of those who use our human language with the temptations that it brings. And in *Philosophical Investigations* he thinks and says the same things about the psychologists. Psychology is barren, he says, because of conceptual confusions. I think that what he has there in mind is experimental psychologists who start from a mythological view of the nature of mental processes, which they take from ordinary language, and accept unquestioned, as if it were the experimental basis of their research.

So much for Wittgenstein's view of the relation between philosophy and the common sense of the ordinary man, and between philosophy and other disciplines. I want to end by discussing something about which I feel rather uncertain: how did Wittgenstein think philosophy as *he* did it and as *he* conceived it was related to traditional philosophy? It is clear that he thought at least sometimes that he was doing philosophy in a very different way from the great philosophers, the traditional philosophers. He often uses 'philosophers' almost as a term of abuse, as a term of criticism. For instance:

> When philosophers use a word . . . and try to grasp the *essence* of the thing, one must always ask oneself: is the word ever actually used in this way in the language-game that is its original home? – What *we* do is to bring words back from their metaphysical to their everyday use. (*PI*, I, §116)

Sometimes Wittgenstein says fairly contemptuous things about philosophers, for instance that 'philosophers are often like little children who scribble a jumble of lines on a piece of paper and then ask grown-ups "what is that?"' (MS 213, 430).

He has a consciousness of a big difference between himself and other philosophers. He says:

> A common-sense person, when he reads earlier philosophers thinks
> – quite rightly – 'Sheer nonsense'. When he listens to me, he thinks –
> rightly again – 'Nothing but stale truisms'. That is how the image of
> philosophy has changed. (MS 219, 6)

I want to end by putting the question: *was* there such a big difference between Wittgenstein's philosophy and traditional philosophy as he thought?

Wittgenstein himself raises a very interesting question: Is there any progress in philosophy? Some people find philosophy the most attractive of all the disciplines for the following reason. Philosophy seems on the one hand to be like a science in that one is in pursuit of truth; there seem to be truths which are discovered in philosophy, certain things which we understand which even the greatest philosophers of previous generations did not understand. So, as a philosopher, one has the excitement of belonging to an ongoing cooperative cumulative process in the way that a scientist does, and one has therefore the hope that one may make one's tiny contribution to the building of the great edifice. Thus philosophy has one of the attractions of science. On the other hand, philosophy seems to have the attraction of the arts, of the humanistic disciplines, in that classic works of philosophy do not date. If we want to learn physics or chemistry, as opposed to their history, we do not nowadays read Newton or Faraday. Whereas in literature we read Homer and Shakespeare not merely in order to know the quaint things that people used to think in those far-off days. So philosophy seems attractive in that it combines being a discipline in pursuit of truth in which things are discovered as in a science, with being a humane discipline in which a great work does not age as in literature.

Wittgenstein would surely not have approved of what I have just said, but he did put himself the question how far is there progress in philosophy. He says:

> You always hear people say that philosophy makes no progress and
> that the same philosophical problems which were already pre-

occupying the Greeks are still troubling us today. But people who say that do not understand the reason why it has to be so. The reason is that our language has remained the same and always introduces us to the same questions. As long as there is a verb 'be' which seems to work like 'eat' and 'drink'; as long as there are adjectives like 'identical' 'true' 'false' 'possible'; as long as people speak of the passage of time and of the extent of space, and so on; as long as all this happens peoople will always run up against the same teasing difficulties and will stare at something which no explanation seems able to remove. . . . I read '. . . philosophers are no nearer to the meaning of 'reality' than Plato got. . . .' What an extraordinary thing! How remarkable that Plato could get so far! Or that we have not been able to get any further! Was it because Plato was *so* clever? (MS 213, 424)

Wittgenstein does not give as ample an answer to the question as his philosophical views as I have described them would allow him to. Even given the comparatively narrow view of philosophy which he argued for, there are various ways in which philosophy can progress. One way in which you could say that there is progress in philosophy, but perhaps not a very comforting one, is the way in which there is progress in the expansion of π. That is to say, mathematicians have made great progress since the days of Pythagoras in the expansion of π; they can expand it to many, many more places than anybody could in ancient Greece. None the less, in another sense, there is no progress, they are no nearer to the end of the expansion of π than Pythagoras was. But there is more to progress in philosophy than that.

Suppose we take first the therapeutic, pessimistic view of philosophy. On this view there is room for progress in philosophy in one of the ways in which there is room for progress in medicine, that is, that as the human race continues and grows older new diseases which were never before heard of, need cures. Philosophical therapy must cure the philosophical diseases from which we suffer, but from which earlier generations were free. But if you take the more optimistic aspect of philosophy as a search for *Übersichtlichkeit* – knowing one's way around, to use another of Wittgenstein's metaphors – philosophy is like a guide to the city, a guide to the workings of language, thought of as a city. The city of languages, as

Wittgenstein says, has many different parts: there is the *Altstadt* with the old buildings, cramped together and not much room but very interesting and exciting, and then there are the great new buildings outside, the sciences, ordered and regimented. As there are new suburbs, so there are new places for the philosopher to guide one around.

But for Wittgenstein there is one very important sense in which there could not be progress in philosophy. This is because philosophy is a matter of the will, not of the intellect. Philosophy is something which everybody must do for himself; an activity which is essentially, not just accidentally, a striving against one's own intellectual temptations. It is clear that this cannot be something which is so done once for all by the human race in the seventeenth-century and then does not need to be done again. It is characteristic of scientific research that if the research is well done, it does not need to be done again. If you have to repeat a piece of scientific research it shows that either the research was botched to begin with or that other things have happened since which place it in a different context. In the case of curing an individual sickness or in the case of mental discipline one cannot say that once done it need not be done again. It must be done for each person afresh: in that way everybody has to start again and there is no progress. This insight of Wittgenstein's seems to me correct; but I do not think it means in any way that his thought is as discontinuous with the great tradition of Western philosophy as he sometimes seems to have believed it was. Of course Wittgenstein was hostile to metaphysics, to the pretensions of rationalistic philosophy to prove the existence of God, the immortality of the soul, to go far beyond the bounds of experience. He was hostile to that; but then so was Immanuel Kant. Wittgenstein was against the search for essences, for a unique essence common to all uses of a word, but so, after all were the medieval scholastics who developed the theory of analogy. Wittgenstein was insistent that all our intellectual inquiries depend for the possibility of their existence on all kinds of simple, natural, inexplicable, original impulses of human mind; but so, for very similar reasons, was David Hume. Wittgenstein was anxious that the philosopher should distinguish between parts of speech, which the grammarians lump together; where the grammarians for instance talk about verbs the philosopher must distinguish within this overbroad category between processes and conditions and dispositions, etc. But almost word for word the distinctions made in this spirit in the 'Brown Book' and elsewhere correspond to the distinctions between the different types of *hexeis* and the different types of *energeia* in Aristotle.

Finally, Wittgenstein's insistence that philosophy is something that each man must do for himself, and which is a matter of the will, not of the intellect, resembles most of all the philosopher with whom he is most frequently contrasted, René Descartes. Descartes' philosophical masterpiece was not a textbook but a series of meditations which each person must go through for himself; the doubt and the *cogito* was a discipline which each person must administer to himself. Descartes embraced the idea that the philosophy was a matter of the will, not of the intellect, so enthusiastically that he said that judgment itself was an act of the will.

In philosophy of mind, the importance of Wittgenstein in history arises from his exposure of confusion which philosophy inherited from Descartes. But in the matter of the nature of philosophy Descartes and Wittgenstein are fundamentally at one.

5

Intentionality: Aquinas and Wittgenstein

In part I, section V of the *Philosophical Grammar* Wittgenstein sets himself a problem.

> That's *him* (this picture represents *him*) – that contains the whole problem of representation.
>
> What is the criterion, how is it to be verified, that this picture is the portrait of that object, i.e. that it is *meant* to represent it? It is not similarity that makes the picture a portrait (it might be a striking resemblance of one person, and yet be a portrait of someone else it resembles less). . . .
>
> When I remember my friend and see him 'in my mind's eye', what is the connection between the memory image and its subject? The likeness between them?
>
> . . . Here we have the old problem . . . the problem of the harmony between world and thought. (*PG*, p. 102)

In this paper I will say something about Wittgenstein's answer to his own question, his account of the harmony between world and thought. But mainly in the paper I will discuss an older solution to this old problem, to the question what makes a picture of X a picture *of X*, what makes an image of X an image *of X*, what makes a thought about X be *about X*?

One of the most elaborate and also one of the most puzzling accounts of the harmony between the world and thought is Aquinas' doctrine of the immaterial intentional existence of forms in the mind. According to Aquinas, when I think of redness, what makes my thought be a thought of redness is the form of redness. When I think of a horse, similarly, it is the form of horse which makes the thought be a thought of a horse and not of a cow. What makes the thought of a horse the thought of a horse is the same thing as makes a real horse a horse: namely, the form of horse. The form exists, individualized and enmattered, in the real horse; it exists, immaterial and universal, in my mind. In the one case it has *esse naturale*, existence in nature; in the mind it has a different kind of existence, *esse intentionale*.

What are we to make of this strange doctrine? The first question that arises is: what is a form? One of the most illuminating accounts of Aquinas' doctrine of forms is given by Geach in his paper, 'Form and existence'.[1] This contains a useful comparison between Frege's theory of functions and Aquinas' theory of forms. Just as Frege regarded a predicate, such as '. . . is a horse' as standing for a particular kind of function, namely a concept, so Aquinas held that a general term such as 'horse' standing in predicate position referred to a form. The form referred to by the predicate that occurs in the sentence 'Socrates is wise' may be referred to also by the phrase 'the wisdom of Socrates'; but this latter expression must not be construed as 'wisdom, which belongs to Socrates', just as 'the square root of 4' does not mean 'the square root, which belongs to 4'. 'The wisdom of Socrates' in Geach's terminology refers to an *individualized* form; the expression which indicates the generic form, the form strictly so called, is not 'wisdom' nor 'the wisdom of Socrates' but 'the wisdom of . . .' (Cf. *Summa Theologiae*, Ia, 3, 2 ad 4; Ia, 50, 2). 'Wisdom' *tout court* means nothing in heaven or earth; wisdom is always *wisdom of*; as Aquinas puts it, it is of something (*entis*) rather than itself something (*ens*). Against Plato's doctrine that the form signified by a general term is 'one over against many', Aquinas insisted that the question 'one or many' is itself only intelligible if we ask it in relation to a general term that signifies a form or nature.

Geach admits that the account he gives of individualized forms does not accord in all respects with Aquinas' language; but it is a most interesting analysis in its own right, whether or not it is to be found in its worked out form in Aquinas' writings. Geach treats Aquinas as Aquinas treated Aristotle – improving his insights,

[1] P. T. Geach, 'Form and existence', *Proceedings of the Aristotelian Society*, 1954–5, pp. 250–76.

tactfully masking his confusions, charitably resolving his ambi-
guities. This may exasperate historians, but it is the philosophically
rewarding way to read a classic text. But in some cases Geach
benignly interprets Aquinas in a way which fathers on him
interpretations which fall foul of what Aquinas says explicitly
elsewhere. This is the case, as I shall later try to show, when
Aquinas' doctrine of form is expounded by Geach in the context of
intentional existence.

Another author who has contributed greatly to the exposition of
Aquinas' theory of intentionality in recent years is the Canadian
Jesuit Bernard Lonergan. In his book *Verbum*,[2] Lonergan links the
doctrine of intentionality with the Aristotelian theorem of the
identity in act of knower and known. In the *De Anima* we are told,
as Lonergan summarizes, that

> the one operation, sensation, is effected by the sensible object and
> received in the sensitive potency; as from the object it is action; as in
> the subject, it is passion; thus, sounding is the action of the object
> and hearing the passion of the subject, and so by the theorem of
> identity, sounding and hearing are not two realities but one and the
> same. (p. 147)

Because of differences between Greek and English vocabulary,
Aristotle's point is easier to illustrate with an example such as taste.
A piece of sugar, something which can be tasted, is a sensible
object; my ability to taste is a sensitive potency; the operation of
the sense of taste upon the sensible object is the same thing as the
action of the sensible object upon my sense; that is to say, the
sugar's tasting sweet to me is one and the same event as my tasting
the sweetness of the sugar. The sugar is actually sweet, but until
put into the mouth is only potentially tasting sweet: the scholastic
jargon for this was to say that the sugar, outside the mouth, was
sweet 'in first act' but not 'in second act'. It is the second actuality,
sweetness in second act, which is at one and the same time the
sugar's tasting sweet and the tasting of the sweetness of the sugar.
(Something like black coffee, which can be made sweet if you put

[2] Bernard Lonergan, *Verbum* (Notre Dame Press, 1967).

sugar into it, is not sweet either in first act or second act, but only in potentiality.)

Aquinas adopted this Aristotelian theorem, and frequently states it in its Latin version: *sensibile in actu est sensus in actu*. But he also emphasizes the corresponding doctrine about thought as well as the theorem about sensation. Not only is the actualization of a sensible object the same thing as the actualization of the sense-faculty; so too the actualization of an object of thought is the same thing as the actualization of the capacity for thinking. *Intelligibile in actu est intellectus in actu*.

The meaning of the slogan, however, according to Lonergan, has undergone a change. The meaning is not the original Aristotelian identity in second act, but rather assimilation at the level of ideas, or, as they are called by Aquinas, *species*. Knowing, according to Lonergan, is essentially a matter of assimilation: like is known by like.

> Its grounds in Aristotelian theory are reached easily: as the thing is the thing it is in virtue of its form or species, so too a thought is the ontological reality it is in virtue of its own form or species; so further, unless the form of the thing and the form of the thought were similar, there would be no ground for affirming that the thought was a thought of the things. (p. 148)

The similarity must be a similarity not at the level of matter, but of form: it must be an immaterial assimilation.

> The senses are receptive of sensible forms without the matter natural to those forms, much as wax is receptive of the gold of which the seal is made. In human intellect immaterial assimilation reaches its fulness in immaterial reception: not only is the matter of the agent not transferred to the recipient, as the gold of the seal is not transferred to the wax; not only is the form of the agent not reproduced in matter natural to it, as in sensation; but the form of the agent object is received in a strictly immaterial potency, the possible intellect. (p. 149)

'Possible intellect' is a transliteration of the Latin '*intellectus possibilis*', which is Aquinas' term for the intellect in its role as storehouse of thoughts and ideas. 'Receptive intellect' might be a more illuminating English term for it. This intellect, Lonergan tells us, summarizing Aquinas,

> . . . is not the form of any organ; it has no other nature but ability to receive; it stands to all intelligible forms as prime matter stands to all sensible forms; and precisely because it is in act none of the things to be known, it offers no subjective resistance to objective knowing.

The substance of Lonergan's account of intentionality, then, is as follows. If A is to know X, then the form of A's knowing must be similar to the form of X which is known, but it must also be different. It must be similar in essence, if X is to be known; but it must be different in mode, if A is to be a knower and not merely the known.

> Modal difference of form results from difference in recipients: the form of colour exists naturally in the wall, but intentionally in the eye, because wall and eye are different kinds of recipient; similarly angels have a natural existence on their own but an intentional existence in the intellects of other angels. (p. 151)

Intentional existence and immaterial existence are not the same thing. A pattern exists, naturally and materially, in a coloured object; it exists, intentionally and materially, in the eye or, according to Aquinas, in the lucid medium. Gabriel is a form which exists immaterially and naturally in its own right; it exists immaterially and intentionally in Raphael's thought of Gabriel. The characteristic of intellectual thought, whether of men or angels, is that it is the existence of form in a mode which is both intentional and immaterial.

I leave Aquinas' account of angelic understanding to those who are better acquainted than I with angels; I want to consider his thesis as a thesis about human thought. According to Lonergan's interpretation, the theory is essentially that the form of X when X is thought of is similar to the form existing in an object which is really X. But on Geach's interpretation the doctrine of intentionality should not be treated as a doctrine of the similarity of forms, but as a doctrine of the identity of forms. Geach puts the matter thus:

What makes a sensation or thought of an X to be *of an X* is that it is an individual occurrence of that very form or nature which occurs in an X – it is thus that our mind 'reaches right up to the reality'; what makes it to be a *sensation* or *thought* of an X rather than an actual X or an actual X-ness is that X-ness here occurs in the special way called *esse intentionale*, and not in the 'ordinary' way called *esse naturale*.

So for Geach we have not just similarity but identity of forms. To be sure, my thought of a horse and the form of that horse grazing in the field are two *occurrences* of the form; but they are two occurrences of the *same* form, every bit as much as two occurrences of the form of horse in two horses grazing side by side.

Which is the correct interpretation of Aquinas, Lonergan's or Geach's? In my view, neither interpreter has the matter wholly right, and a third interpretation is possible which is both a more accurate account of Aquinas and a more plausible account of the nature of intentionality.

Lonergan is not successful in establishing that there is a shift of meaning between the two slogans *sensibile in actu est sensus in actu* and *intelligibile in actu est intellectus in actu*. Geach is right that the same theorem of identity is being enunciated both in the case of sensation and of understanding. Aquinas is committed to the identity of the objects of thought and the activity of the thinker just as he is to the identity of the activity of a sense-object and the activity of the sense-faculty. But there is no doubt that the doctrine about thought is more difficult to understand than the doctrine about sensation, and it is not surprising that Lonergan should attempt to adulterate it.

In stating the theorem with regard to the senses earlier I said that a piece of sugar was a sensible object. This is not strictly correct: it is the piece of sugar *qua* sweet ('*dulce*', 'the sweet') which is the sensible object; it is the sweetness of the sugar whose actuality is identical with the taster's tasting, not the sugar itself. In the case of a secondary quality such as sweetness, it is easy enough to accept the theorem of identity in second act. We can understand that the secondary quality in act is one and the same as the activity of the appropriate sense; the sweetness of X just is the ability of X to taste sweet. (It is related, of course, to various chemical properties and constituents of X; but that relation, unlike the relation to the activity of tasting sweet, is a contingent one). But suppose that I think of the redness of X: can it be said that the redness of X just is the ability that X has to be thought of as red? Surely not: so how can the doctrine of identity in act apply to thought as well as to sensation?

To see how, we must recall that for Aquinas the real object of all human knowledge is form. The senses perceive the accidental forms of objects that are appropriate to each modality: with our eyes we see the colours and shapes of objects; with our noses we perceive their smells; colours, shapes, and smells are accidental forms or accidents, as opposed to substantial forms, the forms which locate things in their appropriate species. The accidental forms which are perceived by the senses are individual forms – it is the colour of *this rose* that I see and even the most powerful nose cannot take in the smell of the universal *sulphur*. Substantial form, on the other hand, is grasped not by the senses but by the intellect: the proper object of the human intellect is the nature of form of material things. Material things are composed of matter and form, and the individuality of a parcel of matter is not something that can be grasped by the intellect. The intellect can grasp what makes Socrates a man, but not what makes him Socrates; it can grasp his form but not his matter; or rather, more strictly, it grasps his nature by grasping the form plus the fact that the form must be embodied in some matter or other of the right kind. But because it is matter which is the principle of individuation, the form which is grasped by the intellect is universal, unlike the individual accidental forms which are the objects of sense-perception.

This feature is neglected in Geach's presentation of the theory that the form of the thought is the same as the form of the object of thought. Geach argues that we must make a real distinction between form and existence: in the case of each individualized form there is a distinction between the form and its *esse*. But Aquinas' doctrine of intentionality does not provide grounds for such a distinction, contrary to what Geach says. It is no part of Aquinas' doctrine that there is one same individualized form of horse which occurs in a particular horse, say Eclipse, with *esse naturale*, and occurs also in my mind with *esse intentionale*. What we have are two different individualizations of the same form, not two different existences of the same individualized form. The form, in the mind, is individuated by its thinker.

Geach writes:

> When Plato thinks of redness, what exists in Plato is not a certain *relation* to redness or red things, but *is* redness, is an individual occurrence of the very same form of which another individual occurrence is the redness of this rose.

There is an equivocation in the sense of 'individual occurrence' here. The occurrence of redness in a particular rose is an individual occurrence because it is an occurrence of redness in a particular rose: it is the redness of *this rose*. The occurrence of redness when Plato thinks of redness is not individual by being the thought of the redness of any particular thing, but by being a thought thought by a particular thinker, namely Plato. It was a constant doctrine of Aquinas that thought, as such, is not directly of individual things at all, neither of individual forms like the redness of Socrates nor of individual substances like Socrates himself (e.g. *S. Th.*, Ia, 86, 1). When I think of Socrates there is no form of Socrateity having intentional existence in my mind; unlike Duns Scotus who believed in individual essence, *haecceitas*, Aquinas would have denied that there was any such form. According to Aquinas, when I think of Socrates there is in my mind only the universal form of humanity; I can use this form to think of Socrates only by placing it within a context of sensory imagery (*phantasmata*). The individual humanity of Socrates has *esse naturale* in Socrates but it does not have *esse intentionale* in my mind or in anyone's mind; the universal, humanity, has *esse intentionale* in my mind, but it does not have *esse naturale* in Socrates or in any human being. In neither case do we have one same individualized form with two different modes of *esse*. So the doctrine of intentionality is not, as Geach represents it, a doctrine of two modes of existence of the same individualized form. For in thought there are no individualized forms, only universals.

An accurate account of Aquinas' theory of intentionality has to give full weight to his thesis that there is no intellectual knowledge of individuals.

Aquinas wrote:

Plato thought that the forms of natural things existed apart without matter and were therefore thinkable; because what makes something actually thinkable (*actu intelligibile*) is its being non-material. These he called ideas. Corporeal matter, he thought, takes the form it does by sharing in these, so that individuals by this sharing belong in their natural kinds or types; and it is by sharing in them that our understanding takes the forms that it does of knowledge of the different kinds and types. But Aristotle did not think that the forms of natural things existed independently of matter, and forms existing in matter are not actually thinkable. (*S. Th.*, Ia, 19, 3)

Forms existing in matter, Aquinas says, are only thinkable in the same way as colours are visible in the dark. Colours are perceptible by the sense of sight; but in the dark colours are only perceptible potentially, they are not actually perceptible. The sense of vision is only actuated – a man only sees the colours – when light is present to render them actually perceptible. Similarly, Aquinas says, the things in the physical world are only potentially thinkable or intelligible. An animal with the same senses as ours perceives and deals with the same material objects as we do; but he cannot have intellectual thoughts about them – he cannot, for instance, have a scientific understanding of their nature. To explain our ability to do so we have to postulate a species-specific capacity for abstract thought: what Aquinas calls the agent intellect, the *intellectus agens* which he contrasts with the receptive intellect or *intellectus possibilis*. We, because we can abstract ideas from the material conditions of the natural world, are able not just to perceive but to think about and understand the world.

Does this mean that Aquinas is an idealist? Does he mean that we never really know or understand the world itself, but only our own immaterial, abstract, universal ideas? Aquinas was not a representative idealist: he explicitly rejected the thesis that the intellect can know nothing but its own ideas. But Aquinas' thesis does mean that he is anti-realist in one of the many senses of that term. And, though he did not think that we can know nothing but our own ideas, he rejected equally the idea that our knowledge of material objects could be something which was purely intellectual. In this, I believe, his instinct was sound, if we identify 'intellectual' with 'linguistic'.

When I think of a particular human being, there will be, if I know her well, very many descriptions I can give in language to identify the person I mean. But unless I bring in reference to particular times and places there may be no description I can give which would not in theory be satisfiable by a human being other than the one I mean; I cannot individuate simply by describing her appearance, her qualities. Only perhaps by pointing, or taking you to see her, can I make clear which person I mean; and pointing and vision go beyond pure intellectual, linguistic, thought.

Similarly, Aquinas thought, if I bring in spatiotemporal individuating references I have left the realm of intellectual thought: from the point of view of a pure spirit there would be no such framework.

> Our intellect cannot have direct and primary knowledge of individual material objects. The reason is that the principle of individuation of material objects is individual matter; and our intellect understands by abstracting ideas from such matter. But what is abstracted from individual matter is universal. So our intellect is not directly capable of knowing anything which is not universal. (*S. Th.*, Ia, 86, 1)

It is by linking universal intellectual ideas with sensory experience that we know individuals and are capable of forming singular propositions such as 'Socrates is a man'.

If Plato was wrong, as Aquinas thought he was, then there is not, outside the mind, any such thing as human nature as such; there is only the human nature of individual human beings like Jack and Jill. But, because the humanity of individuals is form embedded in matter, it is not something which can, as such, be the object of intellectual thought. In Aquinas' terminology, an individual's humanity is 'intelligible' (because a form) but not 'actually intelligible' (because existing in matter). It is the agent intellect which, on the basis of our experience of individual human beings, creates the intellectual object, humanity as such. This, then, is the sense in which Aquinas, though not an idealist, is anti-realist. The ideas are not intermediate entities which represent the world: they are modifications of our intellect consisting in the acquired ability to think certain thoughts. But the universals which the ideas are ideas of are themselves things which have no existence outside the mind, as universals. Their only existence is their ability to occur in thoughts. Thus the actuality of the universal thoughts is one and the same thing as the actuality of the capacity for intellectual thought. *Intelligibile in actu est intellectus in actu.*

Putting Aquinas' doctrine in modern terms, we might say that our thoughts have the sense they have because of the universal forms in which we think; they have the reference they have to individuals because of the sensory context in which they occur. In *Philosophical Investigations*, II, xi, Wittgenstein wrote:

> 'At that word we both thought of him.' Let us assume that each of us said the same words to himself – and how can it mean MORE than that? – but wouldn't even those words be only a *germ*? They must surely belong to a language and to a context, in order really to be the expression of the thought *of* that man.
>
> If God had looked into our minds he would not have been able to see there whom we were speaking of. (*PI*, p. 217)

If by 'mind' we mean 'intellect' Aquinas would have agreed. To see my reference to an individual, God would have to look outside the intellect to the *phantasmata*.

It is not altogether clear what Aquinas means by *phantasmata*: I have been translating his references to them by vague and benign phrases such as 'reference to a context of sense and imagination'. I believe that in Aquinas' dicta about phantasms there is combined a correct and important insight about the relation between the intellect on the one hand and the imagination and senses on the other, with a confused theory about the nature of the imagination and the character of mental imagery.

Aquinas often states that phantasms are necessary not only for the acquisition of concepts but also for their exercise. In this life at least, it is impossible for us to think any thought except by attending to phantasms. We can see this, he says, if we reflect that injury to the brain can impede thought, and if we remember that we all conjure up images when we are doing our best to understand something. However dubious these arguments may be, it does seem to be true that there must be some exercise of sense or imagination, some application to a sensory context, if we are to be able to pin down someone's habitual knowledge or beliefs to an exercise on a particular occasion. He need not recite to himself his belief in his imagination, or see its content in his mind's eye perhaps; but at least something in his sensory experience or conscious behaviour must occur for it to be possible to latch the thought on to a date and time.

Attention to phantasms is, according to Aquinas, necessary for any thought, even of the most abstract and universal kind. But a special type of relationship to phantasms (*reflexio supra phantasmata*) is needed if the thought is to be a thought concerning individuals rather than universals. In a manner which remains mysterious, Aquinas seems to have thought that only the appropriate accompanying mental imagery would differentiate a thought about Socrates from a thought about Plato or about any other human being. Even if this is so, it seems that the same questions about individuation could arise about the mental imagery as arise about the thought, unless we relate the imagery in some way to a transaction in the world outside the imagination. This brings us back to Wittgenstein's question from which we began: what makes an image of X an image *of X*? Wittgenstein's own answer to his problem goes as follows:

> How can I know that someone means [a] picture as a portrait of N?
> – Well, perhaps he says so or writes it underneath.
> What is the connection between the portrait of N and N himself? Perhaps that the name written underneath is the name used to address him. . . .
> The image of him is an unpainted portrait.
> In the case of the image too, I have to write his name under the picture to make it the image of him. (*PG*, p. 102)

Aquinas' theory of the imagination is in some sense naive and unsatisfactory: he calls the imagination an inner sense and his picture of how it operates is modelled far too closely on the operation of the senses. He seems to have thought that an inner sense differed from an outer sense principally in having an organ and an object inside the body (in the brain) rather than outside.

Wittgenstein and others have shown how misleading this picture of the imagination is. If we are to accept Aquinas' view that it is *phantasmata* which give references to individuals, we have to fill out his account with the kind of considerations which Wittgenstein adduces.

While Aquinas' account of the imagination seems unacceptable, he has a clear grasp of the relationship between the intellect and the imagination when thought takes place in mental images or in subvocal speech. In such cases it is not the imagery that gives content to the intellectual thought, or meaning to the words which express the thought. It is the intellect that gives meaning to the imagery – whether imagined words or pictures or mental images – by using it in a certain way. In the book of our thoughts it is the intellect that provides the text; the mental images are illustrations. (Cf. *PI*, I, §663.)

We can sum up Aquinas' doctrine of intentionality thus. Both sense-perception and the acquisition of intellectual information and matters of the reception of forms in a more or less immaterial manner by a human being. In both perception and in thought a form exists intentionally. When I see the redness of the setting sun redness exists intentionally in my vision; when I think of the roundness of the earth, roundness exists in my intellect. In each case the form exists without the matter to which it is joined in reality: the sun itself does not enter into my eye, nor does the earth, with all its mass, move into my intellect.

> A sensory form exists in one manner in the thing which is outside the soul, and in another manner in the sense itself, which receives the form of sensible objects without their matter – the colour of gold, for instance, without the gold. (*S. Th.*, Ia, 84, 1c)

But intentional existence is not, as such, completely immaterial existence. The form in the eye lacks the matter of gold, but not the matter of the eye; it is an individualized form, not a universal. And according to Aquinas the redness exists intentionally not only in the eye but in the lucid medium through which I see it.

But matters are different with the forms of thought. In the intellect there is no matter for the forms to inform. The receptive intellect indeed has no other nature than its ability to be informed by forms existing intentionally; if it had, it would be incapable of understanding whatever shared its nature, as coloured spectacles prevent one from distinguishing white light from light of their own colour (Ia, 75, 2; 87, 1). The occurrence of concepts and thoughts in the intellect is not a case of the modification of any matter: there is no moulding of mysterious mental material. If the intellect were composed of matter and form, the forms of things would be received into it in all their concrete individuality, so that it would known only the singular, as the senses do, which receive forms of things in a physical organ (Ia, 75, 5).

Aquinas' doctrine of the intentional existence of forms remains one of the most interesting contributions ever made to the philosophical problem of the nature of thought. Suppose that I think of a phoenix. There seem to be two things which make this thought the thought it is: first, that it is a thought of a phoenix, and not of a cow or of a goat; secondly, that it is my thought and not your thought or Julius Caesar's. These seem to be the two essential properties of any thought: to have a content, and to have a possessor. Of course, thoughts may have other properties too – e.g. they may be profound or childish, exciting or depressing, and so on – but the two things essential to any thoughts seem to be that they should be somebody's thoughts and that they should be thoughts of something. Any theory of the nature of thought must give an account of both these features.

Theories of thought propounded at different times emphasize different members of this pair of features. From the time of Descartes until comparatively recently the problem 'What makes my thoughts *my* thoughts' has comparatively rarely struck philosophers as problematic at all; but many have sought to give a solution to the problem of the relation of a thought to what it is a thought of. Does a thought become a thought of X by being *like* X? Or is the relationship between thought and its object some other relationship? How can it be a relationship at all, since we can have thoughts of what does not exist, like my thought of a phoenix, and there is nothing in such a case for my thought to be related to. Moreover, even if we could agree on the relationship – say resemblance – and concentrate on the cases where there are things to be related to – say horses – there is still the problem: what *has* the relationship. A statue of a horse is a piece of stone or bronze, resembling, with greater or less success, a real horse; but in the mind there is nothing corresponding to the stone or the bronze to bear the resemblance. Aquinas' answer, that what makes the thought of a horse the thought of a horse is not any resemblance, but an occurrence of the same thing which makes a horse a horse, makes easier the question concerning the content of the thought; but it makes more striking the question: what makes A's thought of a horse *A's* thought? There is nothing in the content of a thought that makes it one person's thought rather than another's. Innumerable people beside myself believe that two and two make four: when I believe this what makes the belief *my* belief?

The question was a very lively one in Aquinas' time and the subject of much controversy between Latin and Arab interpreters of Aristotle. Aquinas insisted, against the Averroists, that such a thought is my thought, and not the thought of any world-soul or supra-individual agent intellect. But to the question what makes them *my* thoughts his only answer is the connection between the intellectual content of the thought and the mental images in which it is embodied. It is because these mental images are the products of my body that the intellectual thought is my thought. This answer seems unsatisfactory for many reasons. Wittgenstein, who reawoke philosophers to the importance of the question of individuating the possessor of a thought, was surely better inspired when he urges us to look at the expression of a thought to supply the criteria for individuating its possessor. Aquinas has nothing of value to offer in the search for such criteria: his significance for the modern reader here is that he alerts one to the existence of the problem.

But, if we make allowances for this lacuna in Aquinas' theory, can we say that in other respects the thesis of intentionality can be regarded as a sound philosophical account of the nature of thought?

The theorem that the activity of a sensible property is identical with the activity of a sense-faculty seems to be strictly true only of secondary qualities like taste and colour; it is only of these that we can say that their only actualization, the only exercise of their powers, is the actualization of sense-faculties. A primary quality, like heaviness, can be actualized not only be causing a feeling of heaviness in a lifter, but in other ways such as by falling and exerting pressure on inanimate objects.

But the intellectual equivalent of the theorem of identity in second act still seems defensible as a formulation of a particular kind of anti-realism. The actuality of the object of thought is the actuality of the power of thinking. That is to say, on the one hand, the intellect just is the capacity for, the locus of, intellectual thought; it has no structure or matter; it is just the capacity for thought. (Or, if we say it has a structure, all that this can mean is that it is a capacity which can be stratified, hierarchically, into other abilities and powers.) On the other hand, the object of intellectual thought, redness as such, is something which has no existence outside thought. Or so we must say unless we are prepared to embrace the Platonism which Aquinas rejected.

Of course, material objects are not to be identified with universals. They are objects which are thinkable in potency: their thinkability, their intelligibility, is their capacity to be brought under the universal concepts of the intellect's creation.

It is a commonplace to distinguish between two concepts of concept, of *Begriff*. There is an objective one, associated with Frege (a *Begriff* as something 'out there', mind-independent, the reference of a predicate) and a subjective one, associated with Wittgenstein (a concept as, e.g., the learnt mastery of a word in a language).

If Aquinas is right, the two kinds of *Begriff* are facets of the same item. The redness of *this* has existence outside thought; it has its own history and causal interactions; but redness as such has no existence outside thought. Redness as such is not something I think *of*, as I think of Napoleon; it is something, rather, which I think, when I think of redness without thinking of the redness of any particular object. The thinkability of the redness of *this* is its ability to be abstracted by the human abstractive power, the species-specific ability to master language, the *intellectus agens*.

I have attempted to combine Aquinas' theory of intentional existence with the *prima facie* very different account of intentionality sketched by Wittgenstein. The resulting theory, if I am right, has the merit that it enables one to avoid the realist idealism of Platonism without falling into the conceptualist idealism of many anti-realists, past and present.

6

The First Person

As a graduate student at St Benet's Hall, Oxford, from 1957–9 I attended the classes on Wittgenstein given by Elizabeth Anscombe in a chilly and dilapidated outhouse of Somerville College. I look back on those classes as the most exciting and significant event in my education in philosophy. Like many others, when I came to the classes I regarded Wittgenstein's attack on private languages with incomprehension mixed with hostility. Miss Anscombe encouraged us to give the fullest possible expression to our doubts and disagreements: from time to time I found myself thrust into the uncomfortable position of spokesman for the pro-private language party. By the end of the term I had become convinced of the correctness, and the profound importance, of the insights expressed by Wittgenstein in his critique of private ostensive definition. The seminar completely changed the way in which I looked at issues in philosophy of language and philosophy of mind: various lines of thought which until that time I had found seductive, and which many others still follow enthusiastically, lost all their attraction and were revealed as blind alleys and dead ends. The lines of thought ramified over all areas of philosophy, but all of them can broadly be termed Cartesian.

One thing which I learned from reading Wittgenstein with Miss Anscombe was to have an enormous respect for the genius of Descartes. Those who accept a Cartesian view of the mind, I suppose, can admire Descartes for being the first to state certain truths with cogency and elegance and concision. But only one who is cured of Cartesianism can fully be awed by the breathtaking power of an intellect which could propagate, almost unaided, a myth which to this day has such a comprehensive grasp on the imagination of a large part of the human race. To those who doubt the power of Cartesian ideas to survive and flourish in the most hostile of climates, I commend a reading of Professor Anscombe's paper, 'The first person'.[1]

Professor Anscombe's paper takes its start from Descartes' argument to prove that he is not a body. The argument, she observes, is essentially a first-person one, which each of us must go through for himself. The conclusion of the Cartesian doubt could as well have been 'I am not Descartes' as 'I am not a body': Descartes might have concluded to the non-identity of himself with Descartes. This is not the self-contradiction that it seems, because the 'himself' here is not a pronoun replaceable by 'Descartes': it is the indirect reflexive, which has to be explained in terms of 'I'.

We cannot explain 'I' by saying that it is the word each of us uses to refer to himself. If the 'himself' here is the ordinary reflexive pronoun, then the specification is inadequate: one can refer to oneself without knowing one is doing so, and in general knowledge of the referent of a referring expression does not amount to knowledge of its sense. If the 'himself' is the indirect reflexive then the account is circular since the indirect reflexive is simply the *oratio obliqua* version of the *oratio recta* 'I'.

'I' is not a proper name. This is not because it is a name which everyone has: that would be perfectly conceivable. Nor is it because it is a name that everyone uses only to speak of himself. Such a situation too would be imaginable: suppose everyone has '*A*' marked on his wrist, and one of the letters '*B*' to '*Z*' marked on his back; it might be that everyone reported on himself by using '*A*' and on others by using '*B*' to '*Z*' – that would still not make '*A*' like our '*I*' unless it was like 'I', a manifestation of self-consciousness.

What is self-consciousness? Is it a consciousness of a self, a self being something that some things have or are? If so, then we might conceive 'I' as the name of a self, and an account of what kind of thing a self was would clarify the use of 'I' in the way that an account of what a city is could communicate part of what is needed to understand the use of a name like 'London'. But self-consciousness, Professor Anscombe argues, is not consciousness of a self; it is simply consciousness that such-and-such holds of

[1.] G. E. M. Anscombe, 'The first person', in *Mind and Language*, ed. S. Guttenplan (Clarendon Press, 1975), pp. 45–66.

oneself, where 'oneself' is again the indirect reflexive. The very notion of a self is begotten of a misconstrual of this pronoun.

If 'I' is not a proper name shall we simply say then that it is a pronoun? The grammatical category of pronouns is a ragbag, including even variables; and the suggestion given by the word's etymology, that it can be replaced by a noun in a sentence while preserving the sense of the sentence, is false of 'I'. Shall we say that 'I' is a demonstrative? If we use a demonstrative like '*this*' we must be prepared to answer the question '*this what?*'; it is not clear what the corresponding question and answer is with 'I'. Moreover, a demonstrative like 'this' may fail to have a reference (for example, if I say 'this parcel of ashes' pointing to what, unknown to me, is an empty box); no such failure of reference is possible, it seems, if we use 'I' to refer.

In fact, Professor Anscombe insists, 'I' is neither a name nor any other kind of expression whose logical role is to make a reference at all. Of course, it is true that if X makes assertions with 'I' as grammatical subject, then those assertions will be true if and only if what he asserts is true of X. But this doesn't mean that 'I' refers to X, for the truth-condition of the whole sentence does not determine the meaning of the items within the sentence. One who hears or reads a statement with 'I' as subject needs to know whose statement it is if he wants to know how to verify it. But that does not make 'I' a referring expression, any more than the '-o' at the end of a Latin verb such as '*ambulo*', which signifies the same requirement.

If 'I' were a referring expression at all, it would seem to be one whose reference is guaranteed in the sense that the object an 'I'-user means by it must exist so long as he is using 'I', and in the sense that he cannot take the wrong object to be the object he means by 'I'. The only thing thus guaranteed is indeed the Cartesian Ego: certainly not the body.

Imagine that I get into a state of 'sensory deprivation'. Sight is cut off, and I am locally anaesthetized everywhere, perhaps floated in a tank of tepid water; I am unable to speak, or to touch any part of my body with any other. Now I tell myself 'I won't let this happen again!' If the object meant by 'I' is this body, this human being, then

in these circumstances it won't be present to my senses; and how else
can it be 'present to' me? But have I lost what I mean by 'I'? Is that
not present to me? Am I reduced to, as it were, 'referring in
absence'? I have not lost my 'self-consciousness'; nor can what I
mean by "I" be an object no longer present to me. (p. 58)

Thus if 'I' is a referring expression, Descartes was right about its
referent: though his position runs into intolerable difficulties about
the reidentification of the Ego from thought to thought.

The only way to avoid the Cartesian blind alley, Professor
Anscombe maintains, is to break altogether with the idea that 'I'
refers at all. If we give up this idea, we must also recognize that 'I
am N.N.' is not an identity proposition. 'N.N. is this thing here' –
'N.N. is this body' – 'N.N. is this living human being': these are all
identity propositions. But to get from them to 'I am N.N.' we need
the proposition 'I am this thing here' – and this is not an identity
proposition.

The kernel of Anscombe's positive account is given in these
paragraphs:

"I am this thing here" is, then, a real proposition, but not a
proposition of identity. It means: this thing here is the thing, the
person (in the 'offences against the person' sense) of whose action
this idea of action is an idea, of whose movements *these* ideas of
movements are ideas, of whose posture *this* idea of posture is the
idea. And also, of which *these* intended actions, if carried out, will be
the actions. . . .

If I were in the condition of 'sensory deprivation', I could not
have the thought "this object", "this body" – there would be nothing
for "this" to latch on to. But that is not to say I could not still have
the ideas of actions, motion, etc. For these ideas are not extracts
from sensory observation. If I do have them under sensory deprivation, I shall perhaps *believe* that there is such a body. But the
possibility will perhaps strike me that there is none. That is, the
possibility that there is then nothing that I am.

If "I" were a name, it would have to be a name for something with
this sort of connection with this body, not an extra-ordinary name
for this body. Not a name for this body because sensary deprivation
and even loss of consciousness of posture, etc., is not loss of *I*. (That,
at least, is how one would have to put it, treating "I" as a name.)

But "I" is not a name: these I-thoughts are examples of reflective consciousness of states, actions, motions, etc., not of an object I mean by "I", but of this body. These I-thoughts (allow me to pause and think some!) . . . are unmediated conceptions (knowledge or belief, true or false) of states, motions, etc., of this object here, about which I can find out (if I don't know it) that it is E.A. About which I did learn that it is a human being. (p. 62)

Most people with whom I have discussed this article find its destructive arguments unconvincing and its negative conclusion preposterous. For myself, I am wholly persuaded that 'I' is not a referring expression, and that 'I am N.N.' is not an identity proposition. I accept that 'the self' is a piece of philosophers' nonsense produced by misunderstanding of the reflexive pronoun – to ask what kind of substance my *self* is is like asking what the characteristic of *ownness* is which my own property has in addition to its being *mine*. I accept that a person is a living human being, and that I am such a person and not a Cartesian ego, a Lockean self, or an Aristotelian soul. None the less, I find Anscombe's positive account of 'I' unacceptable. Astonishingly, it seems to me, she falls into the Cartesian trap from which Wittgenstein showed us the way out.

Consider the sentence 'This body is the person of whose action *this* idea of action is an idea'. What is *this* idea of action? As Professor Anscombe uttered these words in her lecture, perhaps she had a mental image of herself waving an arm, or had the thought 'I will wave my arm'. This kind of thing, no doubt, is what she was referring to by the expression 'idea of action'. But what is the role of the demonstrative '*this*'? It was not meant to single out one idea of action from among other items in her mental history: it was not meant to contrast, say, the idea of waving an arm with the idea of putting the left foot forward. 'This', in her mouth, in that context, was simply tantamount to 'my'. It was not, of course, an invitation to her hearers to inspect her mental images or to fix their attention on her secret thoughts. But since it was not that, could the remark give her hearers any information at all? To say 'My body is the body of whose action my idea of action is an idea' is not to say anything that could possibly be false; and 'this body is my body' is

equally truistic if 'this body' means 'the body uttering this sentence'. We individuate people's ideas of action by individuating the
bodies that give them expression. When we in the audience listened
to Professor Anscombe's sentence we did not first locate the idea of
action, and then identify the body meant by 'this body' and finally
grasp the relation intended between the two. We were inclined to
assent to what was said simply because the same body, the same
person, was speaking throughout the sentence.

But did not Professor Anscombe make clear *to herself* what she
meant by '*this* idea of action' and do so independently of the truth of
the 'real proposition' which she expressed by saying 'I am this
thing here'? Could she then have been in doubt of, or ignorant of,
which idea of action was meant, and did the mental attention
accompanying 'this' remove or prevent the doubt? It is here that
Wittgenstein's critique of the notion of private ostensive definition
becomes relevant. '*This* idea of action' is not, of course, the
expression of an attempt at private ostensive *definition*: it is not
meant to give *sense* to the expression 'idea of action', but only to
indicate its reference. And Wittgenstein's target was the idea of
private sense, not of private reference; nothing in what he says rules
out the possibility of referring to our own and others' secret
thoughts. But if Wittgenstein is right, any private ostension or
demonstration must be something which it would make sense to
think of as being done publicly: one can refer, for instance, to the
content of a dream or mental image because one could exhibit it by
narrating or drawing it. But when the '*this*' in '*this* idea of action' is
meant to mean 'mine, not someone else's', there does not seem to
be anything that could be a public performance of this private
demonstration without being at the same time a pointing to *this
body*. Hence it seems that '*this* body is the body *these* ideas are about'
cannot be a 'genuine proposition' if that means a proposition that
could be used to convey information.

But even in the public case, it may be said, the body that gives
expression to an idea of action need not be the body that enters into
the content of the idea. When X says to Z through an interpreter Y
'I will meet you at the airport at 10.30' it is Y's body that produces
the sounds, X's body that verifies or falsifies the pronouncement.
But this does not drive a wedge between the individuation of the

idea of action and the individuation of its content: it merely shows that the notion of 'expression' is not a simple one. In such a case, the idea of action is not Y's idea any more than its fulfilment is: when we look for the verifier or falsifier of 'I'-sentences we have to look for the primary utterer of the sentence and not secondary utterers such as interpreters, telephones, or tape-recorders. We individuate the idea of action by individuating the primary utterer; and we discover that X is the primary utterer in such a case by discovering, *inter alia*, the sounds made by X's body within the range of detection of the secondary utterer. If an interpreter relayed Anscombe's lecture to a foreign audience, the expression 'this idea of action' and the expression 'this body' would refer to Anscombe's idea and Anscombe's body, not to the interpreter's.

But are there not cases where speakers disown the sounds coming out of their mouths, without there being any other person or body which can be identified as the primary utterer? Professor Anscombe reminds us of the utterances of mediums and of those who believe themselves possessed by spirits. She invites us to consider the situation in which someone stands before us and says 'Try to believe this: when I say "I", that does not mean this human being who is making the noise. I am someone else who has borrowed this human being to speak through him.' Does not a consideration of such cases show that 'I am this thing here' *is* a genuine proposition, which could serve to convey the information that the listener is *not* face to face with a case of possession or communication through a medium?

We should observe first that the possibility of 'I'-utterances being given a verification by something other than the utterer does not by itself suffice to give content to the notion of control by spirits. Suppose that a sybil in a trance says 'I will destroy Jerusalem on Christmas Day 1984'; and suppose that on Christmas Day 1984 Jerusalem is ravaged by an earthquake or sacked by an army out of control. This, by itself, does not enable us to answer, or even coherently to raise, the question 'And who was the "I" who made the prediction?' Consider the clause in Anscombe's imagined utterance 'When I say "I" . . .'. We can only make something of this because we tacitly accept the first 'I' as standing at least temporarily in the normal relation to the human being who utters it: if we set ourselves to obey the spirit's instructions, it will be the next 'I's uttered *by the same human being* that we will respectfully attend to.

But perhaps Professor Anscombe's logical point can be made without introducing the difficult notion of spiritual agency. Imagine two Siamese twins related in the following way: whenever the mouth of Tweedledum says 'I will do X', the body of Tweedledee does X, and vice versa; and whenever something happens to the body of Tweedledee it is reported in the first person by Tweedledum. Do we not now have a case where the body which owns an 'I'-idea is distinct from the body which provides its subject matter? Cannot either twin say 'I am not *this* body, I am *that* body'? And so have we not a conceivable situation which might be ruled out by the 'genuine proposition' 'I am this body here'?

Nothing in the situation, it seems, *compels* us to say that the body which utters 'I' is not the body which the 'I'-utterances are about. No doubt there is little to attract us in the suggestion that perhaps the 'I'-utterances are about the uttering body, but are just all false – though the body which the 'I'-utterances are about is of course the one which verifies *or falsifies* them. But might not one say that what we have here is a pair of bodies of unusual shapes, with the mouth, instead of being central, being, as it were, an offshore island?

But even if we do say that Tweedledum's mouth utters 'I'-sentences which are about Tweedledee's body we cannot, it seems, take these 'I'-sentences to be expressions of self-consciousness in the way that normal 'I'-sentences are. For let us suppose that Tweedledum has a thought about himself which he wishes to communicate to others: suppose, for instance, he has the thought 'I will tell Professor Anscombe about my pitiable condition'. How is he to carry out this resolve? Which mouth will he use to express the thought 'I am not this body'? If he uses Tweedledee's mouth, then that mouth will say 'I am not this body'. But *that*, if it communicates information at all, communicates information about Tweedledee, not about Tweedledum. If Tweedledum uses his own mouth to express the information, then it is not the case that the 'I'-ideas of Tweedledum are always ideas of the action of Tweedledee's body. We can preserve our fiction from collapsing only if we forget that the expression of a thought by uttering it is as much the enactment of an idea as any other bodily movement. If we exclude the expressive function of 'I'-utterances, then the 'I'-utterances of the twins resemble rather the '*A*'-utterances imagined by Professor Anscombe than the 'I'-utterances of self-conscious persons.

Such fantasies, and the phenomena of possession, may throw into confusion the sense of 'I' emerging from a human mouth. They cannot create a sense of 'I' in which, instead of expressing the self-consciousness of the body to which the mouth belongs, it serves to express the self-consciousness of some other agent. Someone believing himself possessed may of course say 'It was not I who uttered those terrible blasphemies a moment ago'. He is not denying that it was his body that made the noises: and we can make sense of his claim. Not every movement that a person's body makes is a bodily movement of that person: but that does not mean that there can be bodily movements of a person which are not movements of that person's body. For a movement of *X*'s body to be a movement made by *X* it must be a voluntary movement: and the blasphemies of the possessed, we may believe, are not voluntary actions of theirs. But in all this it is the 'I' of the unfortunate person possessed that we can understand, not the 'I' of a possessor.

Let us turn from possession to sensory deprivation. Does the consideration of this enable us to sever the 'I'-thoughts from the body which verifies or falsifies them? Professor Anscombe seems to suggest that in a state of sensory deprivation I can think, and privately concentrate on, 'I'-thoughts (for example 'I won't let this happen again') without knowing which body they concern, and indeed without knowing whether I have a body at all. But if these thoughts have a sense, the sense must surely be expressible; and what they say could only be said publicly if it were said by the right body. Indeed, if I can be said to be in doubt whether I have a body, then the sense of 'I won't let this happen again' must surely be in question. Such a resolve, or plan of action, is a plan *for a body*. The resolve is not like 'I will drive my car home now' said when I do not know that my car has been stolen. 'I will drive my car home, if I still have a car' makes sense; 'I will get out of this bath, if I still have a body' does not. For if I no longer have a body, then I no longer exist, as Professor Anscombe explicitly concedes. And if I do not exist, then I cannot be making resolves either. Following the path of Cartesian doubt seems to lead to a very unCartesian thought: 'Perhaps I don't exist, but if I do exist, I'll never let this happen again.'

Thoughts may be kept to oneself; but even the most secret thought must be capable of being made public, and the sense of the thought expressed in public must be the same as the sense of the thought entertained in private – otherwise we could not speak of the 'expression' of the thought. Professor Anscombe has argued convincingly that 'I' is not a word whose function is to *refer* to its utterer. But it is part of the *sense* of 'I' that assertions containing it are verified or falsified by reference to the history of the assertor. That is something that you know by knowing the grammar of the word, not something you know as a result of study of the context of a particular utterance. A public utterance of an 'I'-sentence has a clear sense only when it is clear which is the body, the person, that utters it as its primary utterer. What goes for the public utterance must go for the private thought too, if Wittgenstein is right that there is no such thing as private sense.

Of course, in a normal case, where there is no sensory deprivation, there may be genuine questions of the form 'Is this body my body?' I may see a body in a mirror, or glimpse part of a trouser leg under the table, for instance, and raise the question. But when these questions are answered, the uncertainty that is removed is an uncertainty about which body *this* is, not an uncertainty about which body *mine* is. In the case of sensory deprivation I cannot have thoughts of the form 'this body is my body', for there is nothing for the 'this' to latch on to, no glimpse or sound or sensation. But what sensory deprivation cuts me off from is the reference of 'this', not the sense of 'my'. It is not as if there is an enterprise of identifying my own body, which I can do in the normal case and fail to do in the case of sensory deprivation. In calling a body 'my body' I do not identify the body, either for myself or for anyone else; though, for others, I may thereby identify *myself*.

In the normal case, it is not by sensory experience that I know I have a body; the lack of sensory experience therefore does not prevent me knowing I have a body, and does not prevent my 'I'-thoughts from being about that body. If it did render it uncertain whether I had a body it would, for the reasons given, render unclear the sense of the 'I' in the 'I'-thoughts. Once again, the attempt to provide a contrast to give content to the utterance 'I am this body' fails. 'I am this body' can be given a sense in particular circumstances, as when pointing to a photograph or a mirror; it does not have a general sense as expressing a truth which each of us knows about himself but cannot communicate to others.

The conclusion of Professor Anscombe's article seemed to be this. 'I am the thinker of these thoughts' is not a genuine proposition, but 'I am this body' is a real proposition which answers a real question. This conclusion I found surprisingly unWittgensteinian: the thinker of these thoughts who is possibly not this person with this body seems uncomfortably similar to a Cartesian ego; and if we allow the conceivability of the notion that we are thus spiritual, it seems no great matter that when we use 'I' we are not actually *referring* to any such spirit or self. I have argued that neither consideration of the role of interpreters, nor reflection on the phenomena of possession, nor imagination of a state of sensory deprivation give reason for thinking that content can be give to 'I'-thoughts where there is no person identifiable as an actual or possible utterer of the thoughts. We cannot drive a wedge between the body that expresses a first-person idea of action, and the body that is the subject-matter of the idea of action, because it is part of the sense of 'I' that utterer and subject should be one and the same. Any circumstances which we could imagine which would suggest a divorce between the two would to the same extent call in question the sense of the 'I' in the 'I'-thoughts.

The arguments I have used in this paper are all derived from principles made familiar by Wittgenstein's critique of private ostensive definition: principles I first came to appreciate at those classes in Somerville some twenty years ago. It may be that I have misunderstood Professor Anscombe's article: I am not sure that I have understood it correctly, but perhaps my expression of my interpretation of it may help others to see it in a clearer light. Whether or not the objections which I have made to it stand up, the article seems to me to be of great interest – an interest which is independent of the question whether it marks the conversion of Professor Anscombe from Wittgenstein to Descartes.

7

Names and Indirect Speech

I

Intentionality is a characteristic of mental states which is exhibited in the fact that reports of such states make use of the *oratio obliqua* construction. Strictly, the *oratio obliqua* construction is a method of reporting an utterance. But philosophers are interested not so much in reports of utterances as in the characteristics of a much wider set of reports, namely those of the form 'A *Fs* that *p*' where 'A' keeps a place for a name and '*p*' for a sentence, while '*Fs*' is to be replaced by any one of a set of finite verbs which is illustrated by examples. It is a common thesis that sentences of this form are not in general to be taken as expressing a relation between objects: they do not relate the subject either to a form of words or to a proposition.

I agree that in 'James said that man is mortal' the expression 'that man is mortal' is not a name. I would go further and claim that in 'James said "man is mortal"' the quotation '"man is mortal"' is not a name. For a name is a simple symbol no part of which is a symbol; whereas the quotation '"man is mortal"' contains a series of quoted expressions each of which has in quotation a symbolic function peculiar to itself though different from the function which it has outside quotation. When 'James says "man is mortal"' reports James' actual words, it does so not by naming his total utterance but by describing it in terms of the expressions contained in the quotation and the order in which they occur.[1]

Since I admit this, I may seem to be committed to accepting the thesis that 'James said that man is mortal' is not about a form of words, and to add to it that 'James said "man is mortal"' is not about a form of words either. I do, indeed, accept these theses if the

[1] Cf. P. T. Geach, *Mental Acts* (Routledge, 1957), pp. 82–5, following Reach.

word 'about' which they contain is so explained that a sentence can be *about* an object only if it contains a name for that object.

In common speech, however, there are other senses of 'about'. It is natural to think that a sentence which contains a definite description of an object is about that object. Before they have read Russell, most people are content to believe that 'The Queen lives in Buckingham Palace' is about the Queen. There are also sentences which tell us something about an object without actually mentioning it by name or description. Thus 'James yawned' tells us something about James' mouth, and might be said to be indirectly about James' mouth. In such cases, the predicate, if fully spelt out, would contain a reference to the object in question. In other cases, it is not a simple predicate, but a description, which contains tacit mention of an object. 'The Mikado is wise' might, in this way, be said to be indirectly about Japan. Again, a sentence which reports an event will often be said to be about that event: in this sense 'Caesar was murdered' is about the murder of Caesar.

In all these senses of 'about' what a sentence is about is a particular thing or event. Scandalously, perhaps, there is also a sense of 'about' for which this requirement does not hold. Somebody who tells a story beginning, 'An Englishman, an Irishman, and a Scotsman were shipwrecked on a desert island . . .' will often be said to have told a story about an Englishman, an Irishman, and a Scotsman; though there is no particular Englishman, Irishman or Scotsman about whom the story tells. But I have no doubt that philosophers have done well to close their eyes to this particular sense of 'about'.

Some philosophers operate with a sense of 'about' much stricter than any I have mentioned. In this strict sense, to say that a sentence is about a certain object is to say that the sentence contains a Russellian proper name for the object. In this sense it may readily be conceded that no *oratio obliqua* sentence is about a form of words. But in this sense – so I shall later argue – no sentence of any kind is ever about anything.

If we think of an utterance as being a form of words produced by a particular speaker on a particular occasion, then there is no doubt that both 'James said "man is mortal"' and 'James said that man is mortal' may be said to be about a form of words. Both these sentences are reports of utterances; so, in the sense in which a report is about what it reports, both these sentences are about utterances.

Henceforth I shall use the noun 'utterance' in such a way that an utterance is not a set of words uttered but the actual uttering of the words. If we use it in this way, then 'James said that man is mortal' is about the form of words James uttered only in the remote way in which 'James yawned' is about James' mouth. Moreover, since it does not tell us *which* form of words James used, it is only about that form of words in the rather disreputable sense of 'about' in which a joke may be a joke about an Englishman, an Irishman, and a Scotsman. But the sentence does tell us that James used a form of words which means the same as 'man is mortal'. So it is about *this* form of words in the way in which 'The Mikado is wise' is about Japan.

In this sense of 'about' a sentence such as 'By leaving the tap dripping, James brought it about that the boiler exploded' is not about a form of words; it does not report an utterance nor describe any event in terms of a sentence. This fact has been used to cast doubt on the idea that 'James said that man is mortal' concerns a form of words. But, so far as I can see, all that the argument shows is that there is nothing in the *form* of a sentence of the form 'James *Fs* that *p*' which ensures that the sentence is about a form of words. But there may well be something about the particular main verb in such a sentence which does so. This seems obvious in the case of 'James whispered that man is mortal' and 'James sang that man is mortal'. It seems equally indisputable in the case of 'James said that man is mortal' when this sentence is used to report an utterance.

The utterance which it reports, of course, need not be the utterance of the words 'man is mortal'. James may have said that man is mortal by uttering the words '*homo est mortalis*'. Such an utterance, for that matter, may be reported also in the form 'James said "man is mortal"': English historians who report the sayings of Caesar and Cicero in the *oratio recta* construction do not feel obliged to leave their utterances untranslated. But for the remainder of this paper I shall adopt the harmless and convenient convention of philosophers whereby if an utterance is reported with the aid of quotation marks it should be reported in the actual words of the speaker.

If James said that man is mortal, then either James said 'man is mortal' or James used some other form of words – perhaps even a conventional gesture such as a nod – which had, in the context in which it was used, the same force. In saying this, I am not subscribing to any reductionist theory of *oratio obliqua*, namely, that to say that man is mortal just *is* to say 'man is mortal' or something equivalent. For it is possible to say 'man is mortal' without saying that man is mortal. James may, for instance, say 'man is mortal' in answer to the question 'What is the meaning of "*homo est mortalis*"?', or after puzzling over the crossword clue 'O Smart Milan! (*anag.*)' In neither case does he say that man is mortal.

The relationship between saying 'man is mortal' and saying that man is mortal was explored in some detail by J. L. Austin in his book *How to Do Things with Words*.[2] To say something, Austin explained, is to perform three distinguishable acts: a phonetic act, a phatic act, and a rhetic act. To perform a phonetic act – to produce a phoneme – is to make certain noises. To perform a phatic act – to produce a pheme – is to make those noises as belonging to a certain vocabulary and as conforming to a certain grammar. To perform a rhetic act – to produce a rheme – is to use these vocables with a more or less definite sense and reference.

> Thus 'He said "the cat is on the mat"' reports a phatic act, whereas 'He said that the cat was on the mat' reports a rhetic act. (p. 95)

As we have already seen, the same rhetic act may be performed by different phatic acts. It is possible to perform a phatic act without performing a rhetic act at all. This is done, for instance, by the peasant who says a Latin prayer without knowing the meaning of the words it contains, or the schoolboy who writes '*Balbus aedificat murum*' as an exercise in grammar. But the difference between a phatic act and a rhetic act does not seem to be adequately made out if we simply say, with Austin, that in the rhetic act the words are used with a definite sense and reference. For one thing, as Austin

[2] J. L. Austin, *How to Do Things with Words* (Oxford University Press, 1962).

himself notes, it is possible to perform a rhetic act without referring to anything. A speaker who says that all triangles have three sides does not refer to any triangle or to anything else. Further, it is possible for the sense and reference of all the words occurring in a pheme to be clear and yet for there to be doubt as to what, if any, rhetic act is being performed. When Macbeth reacted to Lady Macbeth's murderous proposals with the hesitant words 'If we should fail?' she replied, 'We fail.' There is no doubt here of the reference of 'we' or the sense of 'fail', but it is an open question whether Lady Macbeth was asking a question, stating a fact, or simply echoing with scorn her husband's timorous utterance. For a pheme to be a rheme, it seems that it may lack reference, but that it must have not only sense but also, we might say, mood. The mood of a rheme is often made clear by the main verb of the sentence which reports the rhetic act. To ask or to order or to assert is to perform a rhetic act: the rheme produced by such an act will be respectively a question, a command, or a statement.

Besides asking and ordering and asserting human beings wonder and wish and judge. Neither to wonder nor to wish nor to judge is to perform either a rhetic or a phatic act: reports of beliefs and desires and wonderings are not reports of utterances. It is of course possible for a man's wondering to take the form of his asking himself questions; for the vehicle of his wishes to be a command muttered between clenched teeth; for his beliefs to find expression in utterances of greater or less audibility. There is also a perceptible similarity between saying a form of words aloud, muttering it, whispering it, saying it wholly inaudibly and saying it in one's head. These activities form a homogeneous series. We might say, with some violence to etymology, that each such activity is an utterance; and utterances can be graded on a continuous scale whose poles are publicity and privacy. We can readily admit that 'James asked himself "Am I in love?"' and 'James said to himself "The man's a fool"' report utterances and are about forms of words no less than 'James said "man is mortal"'. But such private utterances are merely possible, not necessary, accoutrements of mental acts and states.

Not all thought is conversation with oneself, and this has notoriously been a difficulty for those who choose to regard thought as a relationship between a thinker and a form of words. For if a thought may exist without being put into words, how can we be sure that the form of words corresponding to a particular thought exists? And if it does not exist, how can the thinker stand in a relation to it? To be sure, it is possible to believe that thought is a relationship to a form of words without believing that every thought must be put into words *by the thinker in question*. Charitable A may think that B is a fool but never put this thought into words: the words his thought relates him to are not his own, but those of candid C who daily complains 'B is a fool'.

All of us, however, have many beliefs which are never put into words by anyone. For instance, most of us know, most of the time, where we are; which implies that most of us, most of the time, have a belief which could be expressed in the form 'I am in such-and-such a place'. But comparatively few beliefs about a man's whereabouts are ever put into words either by himself or by anybody else.

It seems clear that a thinker cannot stand in any relation to a form of words which does not exist. But it is time to ask what is meant by 'a form of words'. If we mean by this expression a pheme, then a form of words exists if and only if someone has uttered it, publicly or privately. (To avoid unnecessary complications, here and throughout this paper I use 'exists' as equivalent to 'exists or has at some time existed'.) A pheme, said Austin, is a unit of language, whereas a rheme is a unit of speech.

This distinction does not correspond to the distinction between language and speech made by Gilbert Ryle in his paper 'Use, Usage and Meaning'.[3] In that paper Ryle said that a language was a stock of words, constructions and rules; speech, on the other hand, was the activity of saying things in a language. We use the words of a language in order to say things, and sentences are what we produce when we say things, with the aid of words. Words are used, and sentences are made; sentences, unlike words, do not have a use. If we accept this terminology, we must say that a pheme is not simply a unit of language. For it is not just a possible combination of words; it is a possibility which has already been made actual.

[3] *Proceedings of the Aristotelian Society*, suppl. vol. 35 (1961), pp. 223ff.

In his reply to Ryle's paper J. N. Findlay insisted that it was legitimate to think of a language as containing not only vocabulary and rules, but also all possible sentences that can be formed out of the vocabulary in accordance with the rules. This, it seems to me, is correct. Ryle compares words to coins, and sentences to transactions with coins. But words do not exist prior to their use in the way in which coins exist prior to their use. Words are listed in a dictionary, of course, in a way in which sentences are not. But the words are not physically cut out of the dictionary to be used in sentences. The words used in sentences pre-exist as permanent possibilities for a speaker of a particular language; but this is just how the sentences themselves exist. Words, says Ryle, are *used*, sentences are *made*; but the distinction which this gives us is not so sharp as it sounds. It is like the distinction between making and using a path. Which of these you are doing, as you walk through the forest, depends on how many people have been that way before you.

The existence of a word or a sentence is the possibility of a certain use of a symbol or set of symbols. The symbols themselves have to be produced to be used: noises must be made, letters written or marks scored. Within the phatic act itself we can distinguish between making and using: we use the prescribed noises which we combine in the permitted manner to produce the pheme. The pheme thus made we use to perform the rhetic act. The rheme we may regard as the end of this particular chain of instrument and product; we do not use a statement, a question, or a command to construct some further artefact of discourse, though of course a set of statements, of questions or of commands may constitute a narrative, a cross-examination or a decalogue.

If we think of a sentence as a permanent possibility in a language rather than as a pheme which is a particular actualization of this possibility, then provided that a language exists all the sentences which can be uttered in that language exist. This makes it much easier for us to say that belief, and with it many other mental states, consists in a relationship to a form of words. But since a form of words such as a sentence is now defined in terms of possibility, we are not hereby giving any support to the programme of replacing modal and intensional contexts by extensional ones which is often the driving interest of those who canvass relational theories of belief.

I argued earlier that there was a pair of senses, of unequal importance, in which 'James said that man is mortal' was about a form of words. 'James said that man is mortal' is about a form of words in so far as (*a*) it tells us that James used a form of words and (*b*) – more importantly – it describes the form of words which he used in terms of the form of words 'man is mortal'. Reports of mental acts and states appear to be about forms of words in the second, but not in the first, of these senses. 'James came to the conclusion that man is mortal' does not tell us that James used a form of words, for in coming to his conclusion James need not have uttered any words, even *sotto voce* words. But it describes the conclusion that James came to in terms of the form of words 'man is mortal'. If this sentence is true, then those words are an apt expression of the conclusion which James came to; and the conclusion which he came to is identified as the conclusion whose expression is those words. Mental acts and states are definable and identifiable precisely in terms of their expression; and those mental acts and states whose only expression is verbal are definable and identifiable only in terms of the form of words which gives them apt expression. Identity of expression is a criterion of identity for mental acts: if two people perform mental acts which find expression in similar circumstances in the same words, then they perform the same mental act.

In many cases in which a sentence of the form 'A *F*s that *p*' is used to report a mental act or state, '*p*', with variations of inflexion, will be the expression of the mental act or state which the whole sentence reports. Thus 'the cat is on the mat' is the expression of the belief reported by 'James believes that the cat is on the mat'; 'may justice be done' is the expression of the wish reported by 'James wishes that justice may be done'; 'Moscow shall be bombed' is the expression of the decision reported by 'Kennedy has decided that Moscow shall be bombed'. However, in many cases the relationship between expression and report is a more complicated one.

A radical objection may be made to the ways in which I have hitherto been using the word 'about'. A sentence, we may say, must be about the same thing whether it is true or false. But a report may be false, and what it reports may not have happened. No sentence can be about a thing which does not exist or about an event which did not take place. We cannot then say that a report is about what it reports. Moreover, a description may turn out to be vacuous, if what the description tells us is false. So that we cannot say that a sentence is about what is described in it.

It is, I imagine, an argument such as this which leads some philosophers to use 'about' in such a way that a sentence is about an object only if it contains a Russellian proper name for that object. A Russellian proper name is a name which tells us nothing about what it stands for and which can be used only upon acquaintance with its bearer. Because it tells us nothing about what it stands for, it can tell us nothing false about what it stands for. Because it can be used only upon acquaintance with its bearer, there is no danger that its bearer may not exist upon any occasion of its use. If a sentence contains a Russellian proper name, therefore, there is certain to be something for the sentence to be about.

Russell, as is well known, came to the conclusion that the only genuine proper name was 'this'. Wittgenstein and others after him have pointed out that 'this' behaves differently from a name in almost every possible way. You cannot introduce a demonstrative as you can introduce a name, by saying 'This is called "this"'; you cannot use a demonstrative to call, greet, or label a person; you may say 'this man' and 'that woman' but not 'John man' and 'Mary woman'. It seems to have been shown by exclusion that there are no Russellian names at all. But I do not wish to rely on this argument. The conclusions to which Russell's theory leads are so implausible that it seems that no-one would accept them unless convinced on logical grounds that no other account of names was possible. I shall therefore turn to an attempt to present an alternative account.

II

A proper name is a simple symbol whose function in a language is to refer to a particular individual of a certain kind. In common speech, we are quite prepared to allow that two different individuals may share a name: thus, we say that the man who was cuckolded by Lord Nelson had the same name as the man who invented quaternions. Logicians eschew this usage, and make reference to one and the same individual a necessary condition of identity for a name: two equiform symbols are logically two different names if they refer to two different individuals. If we accept this convention, it follows that no two things or persons can have the same name, though two men may have exactly similar names, and the name of a planet may be indistinguishable from the name of a goddess. Reference to one and the same individual is not, however, regarded by logicians as a sufficient condition of identity for names: one man may have two or more names, and most of us do.

According to a common logical doctrine a proper name must have a bearer. If a simple symbol has no reference, then it is not a name. In order to discover what propositions a man knows, it is not sufficient to inspect the contents of his mind. It is necessary also to investigate how things are in the world. For only what is the case can be known. Just so, according to the common opinion, in order to discover which words in a sentence are names it is not sufficient to ascertain the intentions of the user of the sentence. It is necessary also to do some ontological exploration. For only what exists can be named.

The parallel admits of inversion. To discover what a man knows it it necessary to know what is the case. But it is necessary also to know what he believes. *A pari*, it seems, in order to know which words in a sentence are names we must not only know what things there are to be named. We must also know which words the speaker means to be taken as names, and what he means them to be names of. And this, it seems, we cannot settle simply by taking an inventory of the universe. For we cannot, in advance, rule out the possibility that the speaker intends to name something which is not there to be named.

It is customary for us to be told that a word such as 'Apollo' is not a genuine name, but means roughly 'the object having the properties enumerated in the Classical Dictionary'. If a proper name must have a bearer, then, since Apollo does not exist, 'Apollo' is not a name. But when Arruns prayed

> *Summe deum, sancti custos Soractis Apollo,*
> *da, pater, hoc nostris aboleri dedecus armis*

he was certainly intending to use 'Apollo' as a name, that is to say, as a simple symbol to refer to a particular god. If we say that 'Apollo' in that prayer is not a name, it is because we believe there are no gods, not because of any information about what went on in the mind of Arruns.

There are two different ways in which a symbol may fail to have a reference. A modern who uses the word 'Apollo' does not intend to use it as a name; the ancients tried to do so and failed. If we say simply that 'Apollo' is a disguised definite description we fail to distinguish between the two cases. Again, if we say that a proper name must have a bearer, we must admit the possibility of mistake and disagreement about which of the words we use are names. If I use the word 'Gabriel' to refer to the angel of the Annunciation, there will be no agreement in mixed company whether this is a genuine name or not.

It seems unsatisfactory to let what part of speech a word is depend on such extra-linguistic facts as whether there are angels. I shall therefore drop the convention that a proper name must have a bearer, and shall define 'proper name' not by reference to the contents of the universe, but by reference to the intentions of speakers. I shall say that any simple symbol which is used with the intention of referring exclusively to a particular individual of a certain kind is a proper name.

If A intends by the word '*N*' to refer exclusively to B, then A *means* B by '*N*'. Only if B exists will A succeed in referring to B. To refer to something is to be successful in meaning it, just as to win a race is to be successful in running it. 'To use a word as a name' is synonymous with 'to use a name'; for by using a word as a name, one makes it a name. Whatever is referred to, by one or more persons, by the word '*N*', is *called* '*N*'. On the first occasion on which an object is called '*N*' it is *named* '*N*'. If an object has been named '*N*', then *N* is its name. An object has a name only if it has been named. In this way names differ from descriptions: for of course a description may apply to an object though it has never been described.

If an atomic sentence contains a proper name '*N*' which is the name of B, then that sentence is *about B*. If B does not exist, then no sentence is about B. Similarly, a sentence containing a definite description is about what satisfies the description if the description is satisfied; otherwise it is about nothing. If a sentence contains a description which itself contains another name or description, then the sentence is indirectly about what is named by that name or described by that description, if there is such a thing.

We need a word to cover the case in which A uses a sentence which contains the word '*N*' by which he means B though there is no such thing as B. Let us say in such a case that A – or the sentence which he uses – *mentions* B. We have, then, the following scheme:

A believes that *p*   A means B   '*p*' mentions B
A knows that *p*   A refers to B   '*p*' is about B.

In order to use a given name correctly, it is necessary to know both what kind of thing it is a name of, and to know which thing of that kind it names. A proper name is used correctly only if it is used on each occasion of its use to refer to the same object. If I yesterday named an object 'Charles' and I today call an object which I see 'Charles', then I am using the name 'Charles' correctly only if the object which I see today is the same object as the object which I named yesterday. In order, therefore, to use the name correctly, I must know by what criteria I can rightly decide that such an object seen today is the same as an object seen yesterday.[4]

There is no criterion of identity for objects as such. For each kind of thing there is a specific set of conditions for the persisting identity of the individual, and 'object' is not the name of any kind of thing. The conditions for the persisting identity of a man are different from those which apply in the case of a mountain, and those for a mountain are different from those for a symphony; yet men, mountains and symphonies all have names. The mountain I see today is not the same mountain as I saw yesterday if it is not in the same place as the mountain I saw yesterday; the man I see today may well be the man I saw yesterday, though seen yesterday at

[4] Cf. P. T. Geach, *Reference and Generality* (Cornell University Press, 1969), pp. 43ff.

Land's End and today at John o' Groats. We can give no sense to 'being the same' *tout court*, nor is there some single simple relation or attribute called 'identity'; for A to be identical with B is, necessarily, for A to be the same *P* as B, where '*P*' keeps a place for the name of a kind of thing. Since a name may be rightly used only to refer on each occasion of its use to the same thing, it follows that in order rightly to use a name one must know what *kind* of thing it is a name of; since whether A can be said to be the same thing as B will depend, whenever the question arises, partly on what kind of thing is in question.

Besides knowing what kind of thing it names, the user of a name must know which thing of that kind it names. To use a name at all, he must be prepared to give a definite description of the object which he wishes to name. To use a name correctly, he must be prepared to give a definite description which is satisfied by the object which he means. The ability to give some description of the object one means is a necessary, but not always a sufficient, condition for being able to name it. It is necessary to insist that there is no one description of each object, the ability to give which is a necessary condition for using a word as a name of that object. That is to say, the rule we have is this:

> If A uses '*N*' correctly as a name for B, then (Eφ) (A knows that B is the φ-er).

and not this

> (Eφ) (If A uses '*N*' correctly as a name for B, then A knows that B is the φ-er).

For this reason, I would not wish to say, as Russell did of ordinary names, and as Quine suggests of names in general, that a name is an abbreviated definite description. For two different speakers, if they use a name to refer to the same person, use the name with the same meaning; but the definite description by which one speaker identifies the person named may be wholly different from that by which the other speaker identifies him.

On the account which I have given, I am indeed obliged to say that wherever a proper name such as 'John' occurs as the name of a man, we may replace it by some description such as 'The man who is called "John"'. But obviously *this* description is not one which a speaker can use to make clear whom he means by the name 'John'. Nobody knows who John is merely by knowing that he is the man called 'John'. To be sure, by the logicians' convention according to which no two objects can have the same name, if I do know which name is being used, and it is being used correctly, then I know who is being named. But it is impossible to know which name is being used without knowing who is meant by it. In English there are millions of indistinguishable names, each written 'John', and merely by knowing the sound or look of a person's name I do not yet know which name it is. Further, 'The man who is called "John"' turns out on inspection not be be a definite description in Russell's sense at all. It is always logically possible for a description to be satisfied by more than one object; for that reason the analysis of a definite description contains extra clauses to secure uniqueness. But the predicate '. . . is called "John"', by the logicians' convention, cannot apply to more than one object. Again, Russell rightly makes out the distinction between descriptions and names by saying that a name applies to somebody if and only if he is called by that name; whereas a description applies to someone in virtue of what is true or false about him apart from what people call him (*Principia Mathematica*, 67). But the quasi-description '. . . is called "John"' applies to a man if and only if he is called 'John'.

I do not wish to argue that an apparent name *may* not be used as an abbreviated definite description. There are undoubtedly cases where this occurs. If a man uses a proper name, then he implies that it has a bearer, that is to say, that the object which he means exists. If someones says 'Satan exists' or 'Satan does not exist' then he does not imply, but respectively asserts or denies, that Satan exists. It follows that he is not using 'Satan' in these sentences as a proper name. This is deduced, not from the existence or non-existence of Satan, but from the nature of the verb which the speaker attaches to the symbol 'Satan'. On the account given above, if 'Satan' is being used as a proper name, then it can be replaced by 'the devil who is called "Satan"', which can be expanded as 'there is a devil who is called "Satan" and he . . .'. But the man who says 'Satan does not exist' does not mean to assert

that there is a devil who is called 'Satan', and he does not exist. It
follows that whether Satan exists or not, 'Satan' is not used as a
proper name either in 'Satan exists' or in 'Satan does not exist'.
Neither of these sentences, moreover, is about Satan, whether or
not Satan exists.

Any definite description for which 'Satan' might be regarded as
an abbreviation will also be a definite description sufficient to back
the use of 'Satan' as a name by someone who believes that
description to be satisfied. But when 'Satan' is being used as an
abbreviation for a description and not as a name, the meaning of a
sentence in which it occurs depends on what is the description for
which it is intended as an abbreviation. If one man says 'Satan
exists' and another 'Satan does not exist' then they are not
contradicting each other if the description which one would
substitute for 'Satan' is wholly different from the description which
the other would substitute for it.

A Moloch-worshipper who says, 'Moloch demands human sacrifice' would commonly be said to be making a false statement. One
who subscribes to the Russellian view of proper names must say
that either 'Moloch' is not being used in that sentence as a name, or
no assertion, true or false, is being made by the speaker. We need
not take either course. On the definitions given, the Moloch-
worshipper makes a false statement, but not a statement about
Moloch. 'Moloch' remains a genuine name, and so 'Moloch desires
human sacrifice' is well-formed as it stands. But as there is no
Moloch, the sentence is not about Moloch.

To be true, of course, the sentence would have to be about
Moloch; and here we may seem to be violating the rule that a
sentence must be about the same thing whether it is true or false.
Not so. Whether Moloch exists or not, the sentence has the same
meaning; and if Moloch exists, then the sentence is about Moloch
whether it is true or false; whereas if Moloch does not exist then the
sentence is false and is not about Moloch. What a sentence is about
must not depend on whether *that* sentence is true or false. In this
case, what the sentence 'Moloch desires human sacrifice' is about
depends on whether the sentence 'Moloch exists' is true or false.
That sentence, as we have seen, whether true or false, is in neither
case about Moloch.

III

Often we learn the reference of names by being introduced to their bearers. But it is not necessary to be acquainted with an object in order to understand the use of its name. There are many definite descriptions of particular human beings, for example, the knowledge of which will enable a speaker to use a name in full awareness of *which* human being he is referring to. Most of us know perfectly well who it is that we are talking about when we use the name 'Adolf Hitler' without having made the acquaintance of the bearer of that name. On the other hand, it is not sufficient, in order to learn the reference of a name, merely to be told that name while one's attention is directed to its bearer: one must also know, as I have insisted, what *kind* of thing the name is a name of. A man would have misunderstood the use of a name mentioned in an introduction if it was intended as the name of a person and he took it as a name for the collection of cells which at that moment constituted the body of the bearer. One can learn the application of a name only by learning that it is the name of the P that is the φ-er, where 'P' keeps a place for the name of a kind of thing, and 'the φ-er' keeps a place for some definite description which identifies the object named without mentioning its name.

If this is a correct account, then names acquire intelligibility only by being explicitly or implicitly incorporated into a story. If I tell you someone's name by pointing to him and saying 'George', then it is as if I said, 'There is a man to whom I am pointing, and he is called "George"'. The point I am making could be put paradoxically by saying that all reference is cross-reference. It follows that there is no more problem about how we understand the reference of 'Julius Caesar' than there is about how we understand the names of friends we meet daily.

I agree, of course, that if one Mrs Murphy hears one Fr Gordon say that Johnny Jones has measles, but hasn't the foggiest idea who Johnny Jones is, then she cannot be said to believe that Johnny Jones has measles merely because she believes that what Fr Gordon has said is true. But 'A has not the foggiest idea who B is' does not mean the same as 'A is not at this moment enjoying

Russellian acquaintance with B'. If Mrs Murphy rightly believes that by 'Johnny Jones' Fr Gordon means that red-headed 12-year-old from Coronation Street who last week won the Fergus McFergus award for punctuality and neatness, then she is in a perfectly good position to have beliefs about Johnny Jones, even though she has never met him.

If we accept this, does this mean that we are on a slippery slope which leads to the position that if we hear someone we trust saying 'Abracadabra is arbacadarba' then this counts as believing that abracadarba is arbacadarba? This does not seem to be true, any more than it is true that if we believe that a thousand people are a crowd we are on a slippery slope which cannot stop short of the position that one person is a crowd. There is no definite number of true beliefs of the appropriate kind which we must have in order to be said to know who a person is no matter how many true beliefs of the appropriate kind we may have.

Having defined a proper name by reference to the intentions of its user, I must be prepared to answer a question about the occurrence of proper names in indirect speech. If A reports B's words or thoughts, whose intentions settle the status of the apparent names which occur in B's reported utterance or in the expression of B's thoughts? Do we look at A's intentions or at B's intentions? It seems clear that in a world in which not everyone agrees about ontology, if we are to be able to report speech and thought at all, we must be able to do so without committing ourselves to the ontology of those whose speech and thought we report. We must be able to report that someone else used a word as a name without ourselves using that word as a name. It is non-committal reports of this kind which give rise to the phenomenon studied by logicians under the name of 'referential opacity'. If I say 'Paul thinks that Elmer is a fellow-traveller', I imply that Paul regards 'Elmer' as a proper name; but I do not use the word as a name myself, any more than in saying 'Little Willie Williams thinks that Santa Claus comes down the chimney' I am using 'Santa Claus' as a name. In the first case I do not imply either that Elmer exists, or that my report on Paul would remain true if some other name of Elmer were substituted for 'Elmer'; just as in the second case I do not imply that Santa Claus exists, or that, even if in the Williams household Santa Claus is none other than Willie's father, William Williams Jr believes that William Williams Sr comes down the chimney. These sentences, construed with some arbitrariness as referentially opaque, do not report any relationship between Paul and Elmer or between Little Willie and Santa Claus.

In reporting the discourse of others, then, I need not accept their ontology. On occasion, however, I may wish to do so; and in that case I may use a different construction to mark my shouldering of the existential commitments of those whose discourse I report. 'Elmer has been accused by Paul of being a fellow-traveller' commits its utterer to the existence of Elmer and asserts the holding of a relation between Elmer and Paul.

It is time for me to sum up. It seems to me correct to say that we can interpret sentences of the form 'James said that p' and 'James thought that p' on the model of 'James is a man and man is mortal', treating the expression '. . . says that . . .' as an expression comparable to '. . . is a man and . . .'. But it seems to me that we should not *stop* there in our interpretation. We must go on to give some account of the way in which '. . . says that . . .' *differs from* '. . . is a man and . . .'. I have suggested that '. . . said that . . .' is equivalent to '. . . uttered a form of words tantamount to ". . ."' and that '. . . thought that . . .' is equivalent to '. . . had a thought expressible as ". . ."'. On my view, many sentences reporting utterances and beliefs do express a relation, albeit a very indirect one, between a speaker and a form of words. But there are some beliefs, such as Mrs Murphy's, which do not involve a relation, even of this indirect kind, between a subject and any particular expression. It is possible so to report a mental state that the report involves the assertion of a relationship between two individuals. However, it appears to me that the standard form of report of a mental state is not relational because of the phenomenon of referential opacity.

8

Teilhard de Chardin's
The Phenomenon of Man

I

The Phenomenon of Man is a brave book, and demands to be bravely reviewed.[1] Teilhard de Chardin was not afraid to leave the fields in which he had specialized and to attempt a synthesis of all the sciences and the whole of history, past, present and to come. No reader, therefore, is debarred from criticizing this synthesis by lack of competence in Teilhard's special fields. In a project of this magnitude there can be no partial success: a book which sets out to give the key to the universe must be either a very great book or a failure. If one aims to hit the moon, one's efforts must either reach their target or vanish in the vacant interplanetary spaces. Let it therefore be said at once, in defiance of a chorus of enthusiastic critics, that *The Phenomenon of Man* is not a great book. In failing of its purpose, it becomes one further monument to the nemesis which waits on the hubristic attempt to achieve a more than human eye-view of the world.

If the book is to be understood, Teilhard tells us in his Preface, 'it must be read . . . purely and simply as a scientific treatise'. It is difficult to take this remark seriously. The work is completely innocent of the constant reference to experimental verification, the assiduous citation of the first-hand literature, which is necessary to give meaning, let alone cogency, to any sustained scientific argument. We are constantly told, for instance, that 'things have their *within*'. This is put forward throughout the book as a scientific hypothesis, clothed in a wealth of technical-sounding neologisms,

[1] Part I of this chapter is a review of Pierre Teilhard de Chardin's *The Phenomenon of Man* (Collins, 1959) written shortly after its publication; part II is an edited version of my reply to some critics of that review.

such as 'radial energy' and 'internal oscillation'. We look eagerly for an account of the experimental work which alone would enable us even to understand what was meant by 'the *within* of a molecule'. None is forthcoming; instead we are invited to introspect. Perhaps of course, Teilhard thinks that introspection is a legitimate method of scientific observation. In that case he might well have made his argument look even more technical by adding a reference to the occasion when this method was first employed. It would look well on p. 55: '[In man] the existence of a *within* can no longer be evaded, because it is the object of a direct intuition and the substance of all knowledge (Descartes, 1637).'

Much of the book is highly abstract; but its abstraction is not the formalized abstraction of the abstract sciences. Much of it is highly technical; but its technical terms are not those of a specialized dis·ipline forced to expand its vocabulary by the need for precise classification and the use of novel experimental procedures. If the book really were a scientific treatise, it would stand condemned from the outset on account of its systematic use of metaphor and allegory. To be sure, many of Teilhard's metaphors are themselves drawn from different fields of science. (Examples are 'noosphere', pp. 180–4, etc.; 'quantum' as applied to inherited talents, p. 225; 'single organized membrane', of human society, p. 242; 'megasynthesis', p. 243f; 'envelope', p. 251). But a metaphor from science is not a scientific argument. Compare your beloved to a summer's day, by all means; but do not persuade yourself that you are doing science, not even if you specify the temperature, pressure, and humidity of the atmosphere.

If *The Phenomenon of Man* is not a work of science, what is it? A work of philosophy? The suggestion is explicitly rejected by the author; he is not writing metaphysics, he tells us, but 'hyperphysics' (p. 30). He is not attempting to give an explanation of the world, but merely to describe the phenomena, with man as the central phenomenon. He wishes to give scientific interpretation, not ontological explanation; he has sedulously avoided 'the field of the essence of being' (p. 29f).

The reasons Teilhard gives for saying that he is not a philosopher make us suspect that by 'philosopher' he means 'scholastic philosopher'. Certainly he is no orthodox scholastic: on this Sir Julian

Huxley and the Jesuit Casa Generalizia are agreed. But a man who sets out to give an account of the world as a whole cannot achieve his task – if he can achieve it at all – without the aid of some sort of philosophy. For he must concentrate his attention on those very general concepts, common to many or all disciplines, which it is the peculiar province of philosophy to clarify and criticize. Not surprisingly, *The Phenomenon of Man* turns out on inspection to be riddled with philosophy. Because much of the philosophy it contains is in the form of presuppositions rather than arguments, its author is able to deny that he is writing philosophy; but he cannot claim to be exempt from philosophical criticism. Teilhard's work, like Freud's, is not quite science, and not quite philosophy; like Freud's, it is further from either than from poetry.

The philosophical presuppositions of the book are, roughly, the uncriticized assumptions of Descartes. (I say 'the uncriticized assumptions', not 'the systematic conclusions'; for the only explicit mention of Descartes in the book occurs on p. 166 in a rejection of the Cartesian theory that animals are automata.) These assumptions no doubt seem as natural to an educated Frenchman as the closely allied assumptions of Locke do to an educated Englishman. It is this which gives Teilhard the illusion that his work is free from philosophical commitment. He feels that he is assuming nothing which any sane man would not take for granted.

The Preface tells us that 'two basic assumptions go hand in hand to support and govern every development of the theme. The first is the primacy accorded to the psychic and to thought in the stuff of the universe, and the second is . . . the organic nature of mankind' (p. 30). No one would quarrel with the award of a pre-eminent significance to thought in any account of the universe; it is not, however, thought which receives this primacy at the hand of Teilhard, but thought as conceived by Descartes. And since Descartes' conception of thought can be shown to be fundamentally incoherent, 'every development of the theme' of *The Phenomenon of Man* turns out to be a further majestic exploration of a blind alley.

This comes out most clearly in the second chapter of the book, entitled 'The Within of Things'. Teilhard summarizes the contentions of this chapter as follows: 'Things have their *within*; their reserve, one might say; and this appears in definite *qualitative* or quantitative connections with the developments that science recognizes in the cosmic energy' (p. 54).

Teilhard's argument for the existence of the *within* runs as follows:

If some entities display an observable characteristic, then all entities possess this characteristic (even if it is unobservable).

But some entities, namely men, have an observable *within*.

Therefore all entities, including atoms and molecules, have a *within* (even if this is not observable).

This summary, it is perhaps necessary to insist, is not a parody, but a sober precis of pp. 54–7.

Teilhard argues for his first premiss by an appeal to selected instances. We once thought that only some masses were modified by their velocity; now we know that all are. We once thought that only certain substances were radioactive; now we know that all bodies radiate. He then generalizes this pattern: 'An irregularity in nature is only the sharp exacerbation, to the point of perceptible disclosure, of a property of things diffused throughout the universe, in a state which eludes our recognition of its presence' (p. 56).

It takes little reflection to realize that this generalization is inane. If it were correct, we could argue as follows: Some men are tall. Therefore, all men are tall. If there are some short men who do not appear to be tall, this is because tallness is diffused throughout mankind in a state which eludes our recognition of its presence. Or again: Some flags are red. Therefore all flags are red. If there are some green flags which do not appear to be red, this is because the redness which is hidden within them has not yet reached the point of perceptible disclosure. Of course, one might also start with the premiss that some flags are green, and conclude that red flags have an imperceptible greenness. Soon we shall reach the conclusion that all flags are all colours; and then we may well wonder why we bother to have words for the discrimination of colours at all.

It may be objected here that Teilhard's generalization was meant to apply only to the rigorously defined characteristics discussed by scientific disciplines: it was never intended to be used with gross macroscopic predicates like 'tall' and 'red'. But this objection quite misses the point. For it is the whole essence of Teilhard's procedure, here and elsewhere, that the logical behaviour of predicates designed to cope with the macroscopic bodies of everyday life should be regarded as exactly similar to that of technical predicates devised by scientists for the description and measurement of microscopic and hypothetical entities. If Teilhard did not believe this, then he could not even begin to prove that molecules have a *within*.

Let us turn to the second premiss of Teilhard's argument: men have an observable *within*. The physicist's determination to ignore the *within*, he writes, 'breaks down completely with man, in whom the existence of a *within* can no longer be evaded, because it is the object of a direct intuition'. 'The *within*' for Teilhard means the same as 'consciousness': he repeats his argument as follows. 'There is evidence for the appearance of consciousness in man ... therefore, half-seen in this one flash of light, it has a cosmic extension.' 'It is impossible to deny', he concludes, 'that, deep within ourselves, an "interior" appears at the heart of beings, as it were seen through a rent. This is enough to ensure that, in one degree or another, this "interior" should obtrude itself as existing everywhere in nature from all time.' (p. 56)

Here is Cartesianism manifest. The whole of Teilhard's argument depends on the picture of consciousness as an object of introspection: something we can *see* when we look *within*; something which has a purely contingent connection with its expression in our speech and behaviour; something to which we have ourselves direct access, but which others can learn of only indirectly, through accepting our verbal testimony or making causal inferences from our physical behaviour.

There exists a well-known set of arguments, derived especially from Wittgenstein, which show that this picture is radically misleading. To attempt a synopsis of these arguments here would merely bore those to whom they are familiar without convincing those to whom they are not. Enough has been said to show that Teilhard's argument is worth as much or as little as the Cartesian framework within which alone it makes sense.

For if it is to make sense to ascribe consciousness to a mole..ule, then the connection between consciousness and its expression in speech and behaviour must be a purely contingent one, not a necessity of logic. On the other hand, if this connection is not a purely contingent matter, then only human beings, or beings which behave like them, can have consciousness significantly ascribed to them. But Teilhard nowhere suggests that molecules behave like human beings in the relevant respects – e.g. that they emit signals to each other which play the part speech does in human lives. Nowhere does he betray any conviction that they would have so to behave if it was to make sense, even as a hypothesis, to attribute a *within* to them.

If, on the other hand, consciousness is merely contingently connected with its expression in behaviour, then Teilhard's second premiss goes beyond the evidence he alleges in its support. For his premiss was that *men* have consciousness; whereas his evidence was that *he* saw consciousness if he looked within *himself*. How can he generalize his own case so irresponsibly? He cannot look within others: it is the essence of introspection that it should be something which each man must do for himself. Nor can he make a causal deduction from their behaviour: for he cannot begin to establish a correlation between other people's consciousness and their behaviour when the first term of the correlation is in principle unobservable. If it makes sense to wonder whether molecules have consciousness, then it makes sense to doubt whether other men have it. For all Teilhard can say to the contrary, it might be that he and the molecules were the *only* beings in the universe who had a *within*.[2]

I have dealt with these pages in *The Phenomenon of Man* at some length for two reasons. Firstly, their conclusion – that things have a *within* – is regarded by the author as a major contribution to the scientific understanding of the universe, which is recalled and expanded no less than fourteen times in the course of the book.

[2] 'Consciousness', of course, is a word which is itself heavily laden with Cartesian theory, except in the quite special contexts in which it is used in non-philosophical discourse (e.g. in the case of people recovering from faints or anaesthesia). As used by Cartesians, 'consciousness' seems almost to be *defined* as 'what I see when I introspect'. It is intended, however, as Teilhard says in a note to p. 57, as a blanket-word to cover seeing, hearing, tasting, touching, smelling, knowing, intending, choosing, wanting, feeling pain, hoping, remembering, and all the other activities which characterize some or other sentient beings. Such a usage is not necessarily nonsensical, but it is highly dangerous, since it suggests that all these logically very different activities are species of a single genus in virtue of some common quality as an experience which they all share.

Secondly, the argument in these pages is merely one particularly flagrant example of the way in which, throughout the book, dubious philosophy masquerades as scientific reasoning. Similar covert philosophizing could be detected on almost every page, had we but world enough and time.

* For example, on pp. 62–5, Teilhard attempts to establish some principle of correlation between the quantity of psychical energy in the *within*, and the quantity of the physical energy in the *without*, in a given situation. Such a correlation would only be a possibility if psychic events (e.g. thoughts, or acts of understanding) were themselves measurable in the way in which physical events are measurable. But thought and understanding are not processes in a psychical medium as electrolysis and oxidization are processes in a physical medium. Thought and understanding are not processes at all, not even spiritual processes. To be sure, intelligence can be tested and measured; but it is measured by intelligence tests, not by introspection, however painstaking. And intelligence tests take place in the atmosphere, not in the noosphere.

In conclusion, I should like to indicate one particularly bizarre result of the philosophical gaucherie displayed in *The Phenomenon of Man*. Teilhard has long been known as the great Catholic exponent of the evolutionary hypothesis. Now, having read this book, we discover that he does not in fact believe in evolution at all. He believes, as we saw earlier, that whatever exists in the universe at any point exists at every point. As a corollary to this, he also believes that whatever exists in the universe at any time exists at all times. He writes: 'In the world, nothing could ever burst forth as final across the different thresholds successively traversed by evolution (however critical they be) which has not already existed in an obscure and primordial way. If the organic had not existed on earth from the first moment at which it was possible, it would never have begun later.' This principle – which, essentially, is a simple denial of the Aristotelian distinction between act and potency – is described as 'the refrain that runs all the way through this book' (p. 71).

Now, if this thesis is meant seriously, then the universe of Teilhard is as static and immutable as the universe of Archbishop Ussher. The only sort of change that is admitted in it is change of an accidental and comparatively trivial kind – from the primordial to the final, from the obscure to the easily recognizable. But this sort of change ('change within the limits of the species') has been admitted for years by all the most bigoted opponents of transformism.

The crucial point of evolutionary theory as it affected the non-specialist world, the aspect of it which alarmed the orthodox and exhilarated the adventurous, was the suggestion that life might have evolved from non-life, that living beings might have emerged from inert matter. But does Teilhard believe this? Not at all: life emerged from pre-life, the apparently inert matter was already alive (pp. 57, 72, etc.). There is nothing new under the sun.

Teilhard's synthesis is reached only at the cost of ignoring the differences between the elements to be synthesized. This is so whether the differences in question are the logical differences between different modes of description, or the physical differences between entities to which these different modes are appropriate. In an age of extreme specialization and detailed analysis, synthesis is no doubt desirable; but it can be purchased at too high a price. Truth *must* not, and meaningfulness *can* not, be sacrificed to coherence. Teilhard might not agree. 'Truth', he tells us, means coherence and 'meaningfulness' for him appears to mean imaginability. But if coherence and imaginability is all one wants in a synthesis, why trouble to improve on Thales?

II

It may seem perverse to accuse Teilhard of Cartesianism. Descartes introduced a dichotomy between matter and mind, between the 'without' and the 'within', between the world of nature and the world of spirit. How then can I call Cartesian a man who dedicated himself to showing that mind and matter were interdependent, that all things had a 'within' as well as a 'without', that the world of nature and the world of spirit were but two faces of a single created universe? Was not Teilhard's whole purpose to join together what Descartes had put asunder?

Indeed it was; and herein lies the tragedy. The gravamen of the charge against Descartes is not merely that he separated mind and matter, but that he misdescribed both the elements which he separated. Teilhard endeavoured to undo the separation without rectifying the misdescription. In reacting against Descartes, I am maintaining, he remained a victim of Descartes' prejudices. He rejected Descartes' assertions, but he accepted Descartes' concepts; he challenged the Cartesian answers, but found no fault with the Cartesian questions. The wedding which he celebrated, we might say, was not between spirit and nature; it was between two creatures of Descartes' conceiving.

Gilbert Ryle – anticipated, if I remember correctly, by M. Gilson – has nicknamed the Cartesian conception of man as 'the dogma of the Ghost in the Machine'. Adopting for the moment this abusive terminology, we might say that Teilhard subscribed unquestioningly to belief in Descartes' ghost. Only, he departed from orthodox Cartesianism in two points. He insisted that natural science must be concerned not merely with the machine, but with the ghost as well. He hinted, too, that it was not only in human bodies that ghosts were to be found; it might well be that the entire universe was haunted. Apart from these heresies, he subscribed to the dogma which Ryle has pilloried.

But 'ghost' and 'machine', no less than 'within' and 'without', are metaphors. In less rhetorical language, the reasons for saying that Teilhard is a Cartesian are as follows. Just as Descartes grouped together under the name *cogitationes* (*pensées*) not only thoughts, but also volitions, fits of emotion, pains and pleasures, mental images and sensations, so too Teilhard uses the word 'consciousness' to cover 'every kind of psychicism, from the most rudimentary forms of interior perception imaginable to the human phenomenon of reflective thought'. Just as Descartes thought that these *cogitationes* were the object of a singularly infallible reflection upon oneself, so Teilhard maintains that consciousness is discovered by a uniquely indubitable intuition of one's own *within*. Descartes thought that *cogitationes* were merely contingently connected with their bodily expression, so that one could be certain of their existence while still doubting whether one had a body. Similarly, Teilhard thinks that consciousness is merely contingently connected with its outward manifestations, so that one can assert that molecules have consciousness without suggesting that this is reflected in their behaviour. For neither Teilhard nor Descartes is there any conceptual connection between a thought and its expression, between an act of will and its execution, between an emotion and its manifestation, between a sensation and the behaviour of an organic body. For neither is there any necessity of logic that any thoughts should ever be expressed, that any acts of will should ever be carried out, that any emotions should ever be displayed, or that sensations should be in any way dependent on the positions and movements of a body situated in space. For both, the relation between events in the inner world and events in the outer world is a relation of cause and effect. For both, this relation is uniquely mysterious and inexplicable. For both, there is no doubt that the same set of categories − whether 'thing', 'state', 'process', 'attribute', or 'force', 'energy', 'evolution', 'quantum' − are appropriate to both mind and matter.

These assumptions are certainly not peculiar to Descartes and Teilhard. Some at least of them were shared, for example, by Locke, Hume, Russell and Husserl. To this day many people find them quite unobjectionable. I call them Cartesian assumptions not because they are to be found only in Descartes, but because it was his particular way of posing the mind−body problem which gave them the overwhelming influence which they have exercised on modern European thought.

Plausible as they are, and venerable as they have become, these assumptions are not unavoidable. They were quite foreign to the best of ancient and medieval philosophy. Aquinas, for example, went to infinite pains to distinguish the very different acts, skills, capacities and tendencies which Descartes lumped under a single head. For Aquinas, the boundary between spirit and nature was not between 'consciousness' and clockwork; it was between *intellectus* and *sensus*. It was understanding, and judging, and willing, not feeling aches, or seeing colours, or having mental images, which for him set mind apart from matter. The former were possible without a body: God and the holy angels understand and judge and will no less than men. The latter were inconceivable without a living organism; disembodied spirits can neither see nor hear, feel neither joy nor sorrow, have neither imagination nor memory-images.

(*Summa Theologiae*, Ia, 77, 8) For Aquinas, the relation between, say, an emotion and its bodily manifestations was not one of efficient causality. The increase in one's blood pressure when one is angry is, according to him, neither an effect nor a cause of one's anger; it is its *materia*. (*In De Anima*, 1, 2, n 24).[1] Again, when Aquinas used the same categories to describe mental acts as to describe physical events, he was careful to point out the logical differences between reports of the one and reports of the other. If we talk of the mind as 'a subject of change', he insisted, the meaning of 'subject' and the meaning of 'change' is quite different from the meaning which these words have when applied to physical processes (*S. Th.*, Ia, 75, 5 ad 2m). In all these matters Aquinas held views which were significantly different from the assumptions outlined above.[2]

The Cartesian assumptions which were foreign to Aquinas have been criticized in our own day by Wittgenstein. Like Aquinas, and unlike Descartes, Wittgenstein had a keen eye for such logical differences as that between the concept of 'having a pain' and the concept of 'having a thought'.[3] Like Aquinas, and unlike Descartes, Wittgenstein thought that relations such as that between a pain and its symptoms, between an emotion and its manifestations, between a sensation and the behaviour of an organic body, were not merely contingent connections, inductively established, but were built into our concepts of 'pain', 'emotion' and 'sensation'. Like Aquinas, and unlike Descartes, Wittgenstein took endless pains to prevent an illegitimate assimilation of descriptions of psychological happenings to descriptions of physical happenings: pointing out, for example, the change of meaning which a word like 'process' undergoes when used in a psychological report instead of in a physical one (*PI*, I, §§253–75, 339).

Earlier, I presented a dilemma concerning Teilhard's attribution of consciousness to molecules. Either, I said, Wittgenstein is right, and the connection between consciousness and its expression is

---

[1]   The relation between matter and that *of* which it is the matter is not something established inductively, like the relation between cause and effect; it is a matter of logical necessity.

[2]   See P. T. Geach, *Mental Acts* (Routledge, 1957), pp. 3 and 111f.

[3]   Differences which exist even when the thought in question is the thought 'I am in pain' (*Philosophical Investigations*, I, §327, etc.).

non-contingent; or Descartes is right, and the connection is purely contingent. If the former, then molecules, unless they behave like human beings, cannot be said to be conscious; if the latter, then I can have no good reason to attribute consciousness to any other human being, let alone to molecules.

Admirers of Teilhard commonly accept the second horn, with greater or less qualms. I accept the former. Does this involve me in saying that there is no such thing as a private experience? If by a private experience is meant an experience which is not publicly manifested in any way, then I have no wish to deny that there are private experiences. It is an obvious truth that people have thoughts which they do not express and pains which they do not show: to deny this would be manifest folly. It is undeniable that people often itch without scratching or announcing their itch to the public. Such an itch could very properly be described as a private experience. 'At 8.15 on 10 November 1815 Napoleon itched, but he went to his grave without betraying this fact by word or deed.' This is a perfectly meaningful sentence, and is either true or false, though in the nature of the case it is unverifiable by any normal means. Clearly, we could call such a statement a report of a private experience.

Some people, appear to think that since some reports of experiences refer to private experiences, all reports of experiences refer to private. But I do not see this at all. If it is undeniable that some thoughts are kept to oneself, it is equally undeniable that some are communicated to others. If some pains are not shown, others are. If a private experience is an experience which is kept to oneself, what reason is there for calling an experience which is *not* kept to oneself 'a private experience'? If a man itches, but does not scratch or report his itch, we have agreed to say that he has a private itch; but if he itches and *does* scratch, why should we call his itch a private itch? Certainly, in this sense of 'private', not all experiences are private, and if we infer from the fact that a man is scratching that he is probably itching, we are not inferring a *private* experience from a public manifestation.

Now is it a necessary truth, or merely a contingent fact, that not all experiences are private experiences? Does it just happen to be the case, or is it something to do with our concept of 'thought' that not all thoughts are unexpressed? Does it just happen to be the case, or is it something to do with our concept of 'pain' that not all pains are concealed?

Let us point out at once that it does not *follow* from the fact that some experiences are private experiences that all experiences could be private experiences. 'What sometimes happens could always happen' is a fallacy. It might be called the Housekeeper Fallacy, since one of its most painful applications is the argument: 'If you like Irish stew for dinner on some days, you like Irish stew for dinner every day.' Some money is forged; it could not be the case that all money was forged. Some popes were anti-popes; but it could not be the case that all popes were anti-popes. Some people are taller than average; but it could not be the case that all people were taller than average.

If other people give public performances in connection with certain experiences, these experiences are not, in the sense defined, private experiences; and, in this sense, to say that we infer people's private experiences from their public expression of them is a contradiction in terms.[4]

In fact, it can be shown that it is not just a contingent matter that not all experiences are private experiences. Let us return to our itching. Though itching is not always followed by scratching, the link between itching and scratching is not a contingent link. It is not just a well established inductive hypothesis that itching leads to scratching. If someone said 'I frequently itch, but I never want to scratch' would we think merely that he had unusual scratches?

[4]   What other senses could we give to 'experiences are private'? (1) 'Only I can have my own experiences.' To be sure; just as only I can have my own body, and only Kanchenjunga can have its own summit. If you itch, then it is your itch and nobody else's; just as if you blush, then it is your blush and nobody else's, and if you sneeze it is your sneeze and not my sneeze or General de Gaulle's sneeze. But there is nothing specially occult about blushes and sneezes; we don't feel impelled to say that all sneezes are private sneezes, or all blushes private blushes. 'Only I can have my own experiences' tells us nothing about experiences. It draws attention to the grammatical connection between 'I' and 'my'. (2) 'Only I can know my own experiences.' If this is meant to imply e.g. that only I can know when I am angry, then it is patently false. Other people very often know that I am angry; and they may well know it when I do not know it myself but imagine that I am administering just punishment to an offender in a cool and impartial manner. To be sure, I can pretend to be angry; but there can also be circumstances in which others can know that I am not pretending. Note that, if it is claimed to be logically impossible for other people to know my experiences, then not even God can know them. On this view, God could only guess at my secret sins.

Would we not rather wonder what reason he had for calling his sensation 'an itch'? The concepts of 'itching' and 'scratching' are so linked that only something which is the kind of being which could scratch could be intelligibly said to itch.

This is one example of a point of general importance. What experiences one can have depends on what one can *do*. Only someone who can play chess can ever feel the desire to castle; only someone who can talk can be overcome by an impulse to swear. Only a being which can eat can be hungry; only a being which can laugh can be amused. Only a being which can discriminate between light and darkness can have visual experiences; only a being which can discriminate between sounds can have aural experiences.

Now what of 'consciousness'? I said, that only beings which behaved in the relevant respects like human beings could have consciousness significantly ascribed to them. I gave 'emitting signals to each other' as *one* way in which non-human beings might behave like human beings sufficiently to warrant our describing them as conscious beings.[5] I do not, of course, wish to be committed to denying that animals have consciousness; to denying such obvious facts as that cats see, birds are sometimes frightened, and puppies often get excited. Animals behave like human beings in a sufficient number of ways for us to attribute consciousness to them; but they do not emit signals to each other which play quite the part which speech does in human lives.

But there are other distinctions to be made here. 'Consciousness', as I remarked before, is a dangerous word. If it is meant purely as a general term to cover those activities which are peculiar to humans and animals, then it can be used without commitment to any particular philosophical theory. Such a use does indeed bring with it the danger of believing that there is no logical difference worth noting between reports of these differing activities. But this danger can be avoided if one is always prepared, in any given case, to substitute for the word 'consciousness' the appropriate more specific and more concrete description of the activities in question.

Often, however, the word 'consciousness' is used to stand for

[5] I did not, of course, mean that I saw my way to attaching any sense to 'molecules emit signals to each other which play the part which speech does in human lives'!

some feature, directly observable only by introspection, which is common to all these activities, and in virtue of which alone they are entitled to be called 'conscious activities'. If one uses the word in this way, then one is committed to the Cartesian presuppositions; and one is liable to all the objections against these, the chief of which is that there is no such common feature. I shall henceforth use the phrase 'Cartesian consciousness' to refer to what this use of the word is intended to denote, reserving 'consciousness' for the philosophically neutral use mentioned above.

When Teilhard suggests that molecules are conscious, is it consciousness, or Cartesian consciousness, which he is attributing to them? If it is consciousness that is in question here, then Teilhard's suggestion comes to this: that some of the activities which have hitherto been thought to be peculiar to animals are in fact exercised by molecules as well. There seem to me, I must admit, overwhelming difficulties in the way of suggestion; but this may be entirely due to my ignorance of the nature of molecules. However, if we are even to begin to investigate this possibility, we must know *which* activities Teilhard believes to be shared by molecules. Consciousness includes, among other things, seeing, itching, being amused, telling the time, feeling bored, and falling asleep. Teilhard's suggestion at once seems less plausible if we substitute for 'consciousness' the name of some specific conscious activity. 'Perhaps molecules are conscious' sounds much better than 'perhaps molecules often itch' or 'perhaps molecules can tell the time' or 'perhaps molecules find the world highly amusing'. But in fact, Teilhard makes no suggestion as to which are the specific conscious activities which molecules display. He does not seem to feel any necessity to do so. This makes us suspect that it is Cartesian consciousness, not consciousness, which Teilhard has in mind.

This suspicion increases to certainty when we find that it is to introspection, and not to the existence of the peculiarly animal and human capacities and performances, that Teilhard appeals to prove the existence of 'the within'. When Teilhard suggests that molecules have consciousness he is saying 'they have – in an attenuated form, of course – what I see when I look within me'. It is *this* suggestion which I am maintaining is nonsensical.

Am I so intimately acquainted with molecules, then, that I am so sure that they have not got a 'within'? No: it is not out of any study of molecules that I claim to know this. Rather it is that 'the within' means Cartesian consciousness; and Cartesian consciousness is an *Unding* which could be possessed neither by a molecule, nor by a flea, nor by a tram, nor by an archangel. For if 'consciousness' is the name for something which can be observed only by introspection, then the meaning of this name must be learnt by a private and uncheckable performance. But no word could acquire a meaning by such a performance; for a word only has meaning as part of a language; and a language is essentially something public and shared. If 'consciousness' is given its meaning for each of us by a ceremony from which everybody else is excluded, then none of us can have any idea what anyone else means by the word. How do I know, on this view, that what *I* have christened by this name is what *you* have christened by this name? Might it not be that what Teilhard calls 'consciousness' is something totally different from what you call 'consciousness'? On this view, it would not just be that we could never know that 'I am conscious', said by Teilhard, was *true*; we could never even know what it *meant*. In which case, how could we attach any sense at all to the suggestion 'perhaps molecules are conscious'?

To clinch my claim that Teilhard is basing his philosophy on an untenable Cartesianism, I would like to quote the following passage, in which he is endeavouring to characterize the final pole of evolution:

> It is by definition in Omega that – in its flower and its integrity – the hoard of consciousness liberated little by little on earth by noogenesis adds itself together and accumulates. So much has already been accepted. But what exactly do we mean, what is implied, when we use the apparently simple phrase 'addition of consciousness'?
>
> When we listen to the disciples of Marx, we might think it was enough for mankind (for its growth and to justify the sacrifices imposed on us) to gather together the successive acquisitions we bequeath to it in dying – our ideas, our discoveries, our works of art, our example. Surely this imperishable treasure is the best part of our being.

Let us reflect a moment, and we shall soon see that for a universe which, by hypothesis, we admitted to be a 'collector and custodian of consciousness', the mere hoarding of these remains would be nothing but a colossal wastage. What passes from each of us into the mass of humanity by means of invention, education and diffusion of all sorts is admittedly of vital importance. I have sufficiently tried to stress its phyletic value and no one can accuse me of belittling it. But, with that accepted, I am bound to admit that, in these contributions to the collectivity, far from transmitting the most precious, we are bequeathing, at the utmost, only the shadow of ourselves. Our works? But even in the interest of life in general, what is the work of human works if not to establish, in and by means of each one of us, an absolutely original centre in which the universe reflects itself in a unique and inimitable way? And those centres are our very selves and personalities. The very centre of our conscious-ness, deeper than all its radii; that is the essence which Omega, if it is to be truly Omega, must reclaim. And this essence is obviously not something of which we can dispossess ourselves for the benefit of others as we might give away a coat or pass on a torch. For we are the very flame of that torch. To communicate itself, my ego must subsist through abandoning itself or the gift will fade away. The conclusion is inevitable that the concentration of a conscious universe would be unthinkable if it did not reassemble in itself *all consciousness* as well as all *the conscious*; each particular consciousness remaining conscious of itself at the end of the operation, and even (this must absolutely be understood) each particular consciousness becoming still more itself and thus more clearly distinct from others the closer it gets to them in Omega. (pp. 261–2)

This argument comes ill from a man who claims to be systemati-cally restricting himself to the phenomenal point of view. If 'it behoves us not to determine the secret essence but the curve in function of space and time' of spirit, what is Teilhard doing in arguing from the *essence* of spirit to the fate of spirits at Omega *outside space and time*? The 'consciousness' which will be gathered together at the concentration of the universe are not 'variables' or 'specific offects of complexity'; they are persons. A few pages further on we read:

By death, in the animal, the radial is reabsorbed into the tangential, while in man it escapes and is liberated from it. . . . Thus, from the grains of thought forming the veritable and indestructible atoms of its stuff, the universe – a well-defined universe in the outcome – goes on building itself above our heads in the inverse direction of matter which vanishes. The universe is a collector and conservator not of mechanical energy, as we supposed, but of persons. All round us, one by one, like a continual exhalation, 'souls' break away, carrying upwards their incommunicable load of consciousness. (p. 272)

The pretence that Teilhard is restricting himself to a description of phenomena here reaches breaking point. In the passages I have quoted there appears the idea that 'in the very centre of our consciousness, deeper than all its radii', there is to be discovered a 'self', an 'ego' which can be 'liberated' from the body in which it is imprisoned; which can be called indifferently a 'soul' or a 'person'. But this is the very marrow of Cartesianism, the fallacy of the *cogito ergo sum*.

In the *Second Meditation* Descartes argued: 'I can doubt whether I have a body; but I cannot doubt whether I exist; for what is this "I" which is doubting?' It is essential to this argument that it should be possible for Descartes to use 'I' to refer to something of which his body is no part. In other words, Descartes' argument demands that there should be something called 'self' which is only a part of himself. In this his argument is exactly parallel to the argument we have just read in Teilhard.

Both arguments are fallacious. My 'self' is not a *part* of myself – not even a very central or profoundly interior part of myself. My 'self', obviously enough, is myself. I am not my soul any more than I am my body; I am a person, but no part of me is a person. 'I' does not mean my soul any more than it means my body; it means me. My body is a part of myself, and my soul is a part of myself. When I die, even if my soul leaves my body, I shall no longer exist; and I shall not exist again unless there is a Resurrection.

The idea that a body is not an essential part of a human person, so that a human person can exist without his body, is not peculiar to Descartes. It has never been stated more clearly than in the Second Meditation; that is the reason for calling it a Cartesian idea.

It is, of course, open to any admirer of Teilhard to say: 'Very well; Teilhard is a Cartesian. But what of that? Has Descartes' position in these matters been decisively refuted?' But anyone who adopts this position must agree that any discussion of Teilhard's work by scientists must wait upon the question whether the conceptual system of Cartesianism is self-consistent or self-contradictory. And this is a manifestly philosophical question.

9

The Homunculus Fallacy

In the *Philosophical Investigations*, Wittgenstein says: 'Only of a human being and what resembles (behaves like) a living human being can one say: it has sensations; it sees; is blind; hears; is deaf; is conscious or unconscious' (I, §281). This dictum is often rejected in practice by psychologists, physiologists and computer experts, when they take predicates whose normal application is to complete human beings or complete animals and apply them to parts of animals, such as brains, or to electrical systems. This is commonly defended as a harmless pedagogical device; I wish to argue that it is a dangerous practice which may lead to conceptual and methodological confusion. I shall call the reckless application of human-being predicates to insufficiently human-like objects the 'homunculus fallacy', since its most naive form is tantamount to the postulation of a little man within a man to explain human experience and behaviour.

One of the first philosophers to draw attention to the homunculus fallacy was Descartes. In his *Dioptrics*, he describes how 'the objects we look at produce very perfect images in the back of the eyes.'[1] He encourages his readers to convince themselves of this by taking the eye of a newly dead man, replacing with paper or eggshell the enveloping membranes at the back, and placing it inside a shutter so as to let light through it into an otherwise dark room. 'You will see (I dare say with surprise and pleasure) a picture representing in natural perspective all the objects outside.' 'You cannot doubt', he continues, 'that a quite similar picture is produced in a living man's eye, on the lining membrane ... Further, the images are not only produced in the back of the eye

[1] R. Descartes, 'Dioptrics', in *Philosophical Writings*, tr. and ed. E. Anscombe and P. T. Geach (Nelson, 1954), pp. 239–56, at p. 244.

but also sent on to the brain . . . and when it is thus transmitted to the inside of our head, the picture still retains some degree of its resemblance to the objects from which it originates.' But he concludes with a warning. 'We must not think that it is by means of this resemblance that the picture makes us aware of the objects – as though we had another pair of eyes to see it, inside our brain.' (pp. 245–6)

To think of the brain as having eyes and seeing the retinal image would be one way of committing the homunculus fallacy. But in spite of warning us against the fallacy at this point, Descartes himself commits it when he comes to discuss the relationship between the soul and the pineal gland:

> If we see some animal approach us, the light reflected from its body depicts two images of it, one in each of our eyes, and these two images form two others, by means of the optic nerves, in the interior surface of the brain which faces its cavities; then from there, by means of the animal spirits with which its cavities are filled, these images so radiate towards the little gland which is surrounded by these spirits, that the movement which forms each point of one of the images tends towards the same point of the gland towards which tends the movement which forms the point of the other image which represents the same part of this animal. By this means the two images which are in the brain form but one upon the gland, which, acting immediately upon the soul, causes it to see the form of this animal.[2]

To speak of the soul encountering images in the pineal gland is to commit the homunculus fallacy; for *pace* Descartes, a soul is no more a complete human being than a brain is. In itself, there is nothing philosophically incorrect in speaking of images in the brain: Descartes himself is anxious to explain that they are very schematic images and not pictures except in a metaphorical sense:

> No images have to resemble the objects they represent in all respects . . . resemblance in a few features is enough, and very often the perfection of an image depends on its not resembling the object as

---

[2] R. Descartes, 'Passions of the Soul', in *The Philosophical Works of Descartes*, I, tr. and ed. E. S. Haldane and G. R. T. Ross (Constable, 1931), pp. 329–429, at p. 348.

much as it might. For instance, engravings, which consist merely of
a little ink spread over paper, represent to us forests, towns, men and
even battles and tempests. (*Dioptrics*, pp. 246)

There would be nothing philosophically objectionable in the
suggestion that these schematic images might be observed by a
brain surgeon investigating the gland. What is misleading is the
suggestion that these images are visible to the *soul*, whose perception of them constitutes seeing. What is wrong is that exactly the
same sorts of problems arise about Descartes' explanation as about
his *explicandum*. To the Aristotelians who preceded Descartes,
seeing necessitated a non-mechanistic phenomenon taking place in
the eye. Descartes introduced new mechanisms, but in his system
the non-mechanistic event in the eye is replaced by a new
non-mechanistic reading of patterns in the pineal gland. The
interaction between mind and matter is philosophically as puzzling
a few inches behind the eye as it is in the eye itself.

One danger, then, of the homunculus fallacy is that in problems
concerning perception and kindred matters it conceals what is left
to be explained. In the case of Descartes, we are put on our guard
by the quaintness of some of the physiology, so that we have no
difficulty in discovering the gaps in his account; but the philosophical hiatus can coexist with much more sophisticated physiological information.

A contemporary expert on perception, Professor R. L. Gregory,
at the beginning of his book *The Eye and the Brain*, echoes Descartes'
warning against the homunculus fallacy:

> We are so familiar with seeing, that it takes a leap of imagination to
> realize that there are problems to be solved. But consider it. We are
> given tiny distorted upside-down images in the eyes, and we see
> separate solid objects in surrounding space. From the patterns of
> stimulation on the retinas we perceive the world of objects, and this
> is nothing short of a miracle.
>
> The eye is often described as like a camera, but it is the quite
> uncamera-like features of perception which are most interesting.
> How is information from the eyes coded into neural terms, into the
> language of the brain, and reconstituted into experience of sur-
> rounding objects? The task of eye and brain is quite different from

either a photographic or a television camera converting objects merely into images. There is a temptation, which must be avoided, to say that the eyes produce pictures in the brain. A picture in the brain suggests the need of some kind of internal eye to see it but this would need a further eye to see *its* picture . . . and so on in an endless regress of eyes and pictures. This is absurd. What the eyes do is to feed the brain with information coded into neural activity – chains of electrical impulses – which by their code and the patterns of brain activity, represent objects. We may take an analogy from written language; the letters and words on this page have certain meanings, to those who know the language. They affect the reader's brain appropriately, but they are not pictures. When we look at something, the pattern of neural activity represents the objects and to the brain *is* the object. No internal picture is involved.[3]

The warning against the fallacy is excellent; but the fallacy is itself implied in the suggestion that the brain knows a language and that it has an object like the objects of perception. A converse fallacy is committed when it is said that we are given tiny, distorted, upside-down images in the eyes and that we perceive patterns of stimulation on the retina. Here it is not a bogus subject of perception which is being supplied, but a bogus object of perception.

The reader may feel that this is completely unfair criticism. The words I have criticized are taken from the first page of a popular book. What is the harm in personifying parts of the body in order to dramatize scientific information which can be stated in completely neutral metaphor-free language?

Whether dramatization is good pedagogy depends on whether the important events happen on or off stage. The overall psychological problem of perception could be stated as follows: how does a human being cope with the available sensory information, and how does he act on it? Or, in one of Gregory's own formulations, how does information control behaviour? Now this is a problem which would still remain to be solved even if we knew every detail of the process of collection and storage of information; and one crucial aspect of it is the same whether the information is in the world, in the retinas, or in the CNS. The problem is this: what it the relation

[3] R. L. Gregory, *The Eye and the Brain* (McGraw-Hill, 1966), p. 7.

between the presence of information in the technical sense of communication theory and the possession of information in the non-technical sense in which one can acquire information about the world by looking?

For if having information is the same as knowing, then containing information is not the same as having information. An airline schedule contains the information about airline departures; but the airline schedule does not *know* the time of departures of the flights. The illiterate slave on whose shaven scalp the tyrant has tattooed his state secrets does not *know* the information which his head contains.

A category difference is involved here. To contain information is to be in a certain state, while to know something is to possess a certain capacity. A state (such as being a certain shape or size, or having a certain multiplicity or mathematical structure) is something describable by its internal properties; a capacity (such as the ability to run a four minute mile or to speak French) is describable only by specification of what would count as the exercise of the capacity. States and capacities are of course connected: in the simplest case there is an obvious connection between being a round peg (state) and being able to fit into a round hole (capacity). But the connections are not always (as in that case) analytic; and many forms of expertise consist in knowing which states go with which capacities (e.g. what types of mushroom are poisonous, which alloys will stand which strains).

Knowledge is not a state but a capacity, and a capacity of a unique kind. The state of containing certain information is no doubt connected with the capacity which is knowledge of a certain fact; but the two are not identical as the earlier examples show. We may wonder what extra is involved in the knowing that p over and above containing the information that p. .What is knowing a capacity to do, and what counts as an exercise of that capacity? Clearly, there is no simple answer. One cannot specify behaviour typical of knowing as one can specify behaviour typical of anger. One cannot even specify behaviour typical of knowing that p, for a given p; what behaviour the knowledge that p will lead to will depend on what one wants. For instance, knowledge that the window is open will lead to different behaviour in the case of someone who wants it open and in the case of someone who wants it shut. To be sure, the verbal utterance of '*p*' is an activity which is uniquely expressive of the knowledge or belief that *p*; but even so, this does not at all mean that anyone who knows that *p* will ever say that *p*.

There is, then, no simple way of specifying how knowledge gets expressed in behaviour and why some pieces of knowledge do not seem to affect one's behaviour at all. Still, to know is to have the ability to modify one's behaviour in indefinite ways relevant to the pursuit of one's goals. It is because the airline schedule does not have any behaviour to be modified by what is written on it that it does not know what the flight times are.

Let us return from knowing to seeing. Seeing, when not illusory, involves knowing: vision might be defined, crudely, circularly, but not uninformatively, as the acquisition of knowledge in the visual mode. In the Aristotelian tradition, prior to Descartes, it used to be said that it was not the eye that saw, nor the soul, but the whole organism. This was because the normal way to discover whether an organism sees is not just to study its eyes, but to investigate whether its behaviour is affected by changes of light and colour, etc. Consequently, an explanation of seeing must be an explanation not only of the acquisition and storage of information, but also of what makes the containing of this information into knowledge – i.e. its relation to behaviour.

In his paper 'On how so little information controls so much behaviour', Gregory well says:

> Perhaps the most fundamental question in the whole field of experimental psychology is: how far is behaviour controlled by currently available sensory information, and how far by information already stored in the central nervous system?[4]

But in that paper he presents a theory of seeing as selection of internal models without saying how the internal models are related

[4] R. L. Gregory, 'On how so little information controls so much behaviour', Bionics Research Reports, no. 1, April 1968, p. 1. (This paper was also published in *Towards a Theoretical Biology*, II, ed. C. H. Waddington (Edinburgh University Press, 1969), pp. 236–46.)

to behaviour. He speaks of a model 'calling up the appropriate muscle power' for lifting a certain weight, and of models 'mediating appropriate behaviour' (p. 8), but he nowhere shows how these metaphors might be turned into literal language. What he really explains is how information of a certain type might reach the brain.

Now let us suppose that his explanation of this proves completely correct. Even so, the crucial problem remains; and what is still to be done is masked for the reader, if not for Gregory himself, by the use of homunculus predicates of the brain and the use of intentional or representational or symbolic predicates of items in the brain. Consider the following passage from the same paper:

> In general the eye's images are biologically important only in so far as non-optical features can be read from the internal models they select. Images are merely patches of light – which cannot be eaten or be dangerous – but they serve as symbols for selecting internal models, which include the non-visual features vital to survival. It is this reading of object characteristics from images that *is* visual perception. (p. 5)

But even if this mechanism is essential for visual perception, it is not visual perception. Selection of internal models would be possible, as seeing would not, in an isolated optical system incapable of behaviour. This is not just the ordinary language point – 'we wouldn't *call* such a thing seeing' – it is a methodological point concerning the nature of the problems to be solved and the reasonableness of extrapolations from acquired results. The illusion that what is described is visual perception is encouraged by the use of language such as 'features can be *read*' and '*symbols* for selecting'.

Later in the same paper Gregory writes:

> On this general view perception is not directly of sensory information but rather of the internal models selected by sensory information. Indeed the current perception is the prevailing set of models. (p. 8)

Clearly, it is inadequate to explain what perception is by saying that it is perception not of X but of Y: if I wonder what *perception* is, how am I helped by being told that it is of Y rather than of X?

Gregory senses this: that is why his first statement of this thesis is followed by 'indeed' followed by a statement of an incompatible thesis. Perception cannot both be *of* the models and be the models.

So far my objection to the homunculus model has been that it is pedagogically and methodologically dangerous, as helping to cloak the nature of problems to be solved. But there is a more dangerous effect of the model which alone really deserves the name 'fallacy'.

Let us suppose that we waive our objections to the use of human-being predicates for non-human-beings like brains. Let us allow it to be said that the brain is *P*, where *P* is some predicate whose natural application is to whole human beings. (It may, after all, be used in quotes. It usually is – the first time.) There is still an important temptation to be resisted: the temptation to argue from

This man is *P*
to This man's brain is *P*

or *vice versa*. Gregory does not always resist this temptation. At the beginning of the quoted paper he argues that learning or storing particular events is always ontogenetic. Naturally stored information, he says, has two origins: ancestral disasters, and previous experience of the individual stored as 'memory' (p. 1, his quotes). To prove that storage of particular events is always ontogenetic, he says:

> What is certain is that information gained phylogenetically is always of the general 'skill' kind. We are not able to recall individual events experienced by our ancestors. (p. 1)

And *à propos* of learning skills such as tennis and piano playing, he says:

> We may be able to recall the odd particular games or concerts, but as skills it is not individual past events which are stored, but rather appropriate behaviour and strategies. (p. 1)

Here the homunculus fallacy is committed thus: 'X remembers that *p*' is being treated as equivalent to 'X has stored the event that *p'*. The only reason given for saying that information about particular events is not stored phylogenetically is that we cannot recall individual events in our ancestors' lives. But this is to argue from 'this man is not *P*' to 'this man's brain is not *P*' which is fallacious, even if the man's brain's being *P* is a necessary condition for his own being *P*.

In another paper, 'Perceptual illusions and brain models', Gregory considers whether the brain is best regarded as a digital or as an analogue device. He writes:

> It is most implausible to suppose that the brain of a child contains mathematical analyses of physical situations. When a child builds a house of toy bricks, balancing them to make walls and towers, we cannot suppose that the structural problems are solved by employing analytical mathematical techniques, involving concepts such as centre of gravity and coefficient of friction of masses. It is far better to make the lesser claim for children and animals: that they behave appropriately to objects by using analogues of senses object-properties, without involving mathematical analyses of the properties of objects and their interactions. Perceptual learning surely cannot require the learning of mathematics. It is far more plausible to suppose that it involves the building of quite simple analogues of relevant properties of objects: relevant so far as they concern the behaviour of the animal or the child.[5]

Here the homunculus fallacy is committed in the sentence, 'Perceptual learning surely cannot require the learning of mathematics'. It is the child that is doing the perceptual learning; what, if anything, is supposed to be learning mathematics is the child's brain. It is implausible that a child building toy bricks should know advanced mathematics; but from this nothing at all follows about what information is contained in the child's brain.

I conclude that there is good reason to heed the warning of Wittgenstein with which this paper began. The moral is not that the human-being predicates cannot have their use extended at all, but that they must be extended cautiously and self-consciously, and that if they are extended one may not argue from the application of

---

[5] R. L. Gregory, 'Perceptual illusions and brain models', *Proceedings of the Royal Society B*, 171 (1968), pp. 279–96, at p. 294.

such a predicate to a whole human being to the application of the transferred predicate to anything other than the whole human being.

In a brief postscript, I wish to classify some of the points made above, and to disown some of the theses attributed to me by some of those who read that part of this essay. First, I do not accuse Professor Gregory of mistaking mechanistic description for conceptual analysis; nor do I think that either the philosopher's answer or the neurophysiologist's answer to the question 'what is perception?' enjoys a privileged status. Secondly, I do not object to every extension of the application of a predicate from a sentient whole to its parts. Thirdly, I took up no position on the general question whether conscious activities can be said to *be* (nothing but) the micro-structural processes postulated to explain them. I will expand each of these points, and then briefly restate why I call the homunculus fallacy a fallacy.

I do not think that Gregory is under any illusion that he is doing conceptual analysis. I think he is engaged in constructing, and testing experimentally, hypotheses about the mechanisms necessary to explain the phenomena of visual perception. But conceptual analysis is relevant to what he is doing in two ways. First, analysis of the concept of *perception* is necessary to delimit what are the phenomena to be explained; secondly, analysis of the concepts of *sight* and *language* show that such things as seeing and decoding cannot be done by brains unless we can attribute to brains certain types of behaviour which we can attribute to whole human beings. To attribute such activities to brains without suggesting how the relevant behaviour might be attributable to brains is, I maintained, to mask empirical problems which remain to be solved.

The moral of my paper, I said, was not that human-being predicates cannot have their use extended at all, but that their use must be extended cautiously. Consequently, I am unmoved if it is pointed out that hands can grasp and hold: such extensions seem to me well within the bounds of caution. Moreover, my objection was not essentially to predicates of wholes being attached to predicates of parts, but to predicates belonging to human beings being attached to non-human beings. The same fallacy could be committed (though my name for it would not be apt) by the incautious application of human-being predicates to wholes of which human beings are parts, such as communities and states. Populations, like human beings, grow and shrink; but it would obviously be fallacious to argue that a human being was shrinking because the population he belongs to is shrinking, or that a population is growing because every member of it is growing. And states may have intentions which none of their citizens have. (Cf. Wittgenstein, *Zettel*, pp. 1–48.)

The question whether perception can be said to be *identical* with physiological processes seems to me to lack a clear sense, and I do not wish to answer it one way or the other. My complaint against Gregory's identification of visual perception with his postulated selection of internal models was not based on a general thesis that perception cannot be identical with a brain process. Though states and capacities are conceptually different, it need not be misleading to say, e.g. that a peg's ability to fit into round holes *is* its roundness. In the same way, it may be that there is a physiological process – the acquisition of a physiological state – which can be said to *be* visual perception. But no one can claim to have identified such a process until he has brought out its connection with the types of behaviour which are the criteria for the occurrence of visual perception. And this Gregory has not done.

A fallacy, strictly speaking, is a form of argument which can lead from true premises to a false conclusion. The inappropriate use of predicates, not being a form of argument, is not strictly a fallacy, as I observed in my paper. But it leads to a form of argument, which I claimed to detect in Gregory's articles, which *is* fallacious in the strict sense of the word: the argument that because a certain human-being predicate attaches to a human being it attaches to his brain, or *vice versa*. The mere inappropriate use of human-being predicates may be called a fallacy in an extended sense, because it may suggest conclusions which are unjustified; notably the conclusion that more has been explained by a psychological theory than has in fact been explained.

Normally, in an adult human being, the ability to see carries with it the ability to say what is seen, though of course not everything which is actually seen is actually talked about. The use of language to report what is seen, like any use of language, is remarkably free from stimulus control – a point which has been repeatedly made, in general terms, by Chomsky. No account of human perception can approach adequacy unless it includes an explanation of this fact. Consequently, even if we knew every detail of physiological processes by which visual information reaches the brain, and every detail of the physiological processes by which the linguistic utterance of visual reports is produced, the problem of the relationship between the input and the output would be completely untouched. This problem is a major part of the problem of the physiological explanation of perception, and its existence is masked by talk of the brain reading features of objects from images and calling up appropriate muscle power.

10

Language and the Mind

> We may usefully think of the language faculty, the number faculty, and others, as 'mental organs', analogous to the heart or the visual system or the system of motor coordination and planning. There appears to be no clear demarcation line between physical organs, perceptual and motor systems, and cognitive faculties in the respects in question.[1]

To view the language faculty as an organ like the heart involves a deep philosophical confusion. Chomsky's description of the mental structures that he investigates introduces an irrelevant metaphysical element at the interface between physiology and psychology. I intend to justify this complaint by a detailed examination of some crucial passages in Chomsky's latest book, *Rules and Representations*. But before doing so let me, in order to avert misunderstanding, list a number of points on which philosophers have picked quarrels with Chomsky and on which I think it is he, and not his philosophical critics, who is in the right.

I have no quarrel with the idea that there are faculties of the mind, and that the mind in that sense has a modular structure. I have no quarrel with the notion of deep structures, or mental representations, in the only sense in which these are really relevant to the exciting empirical inquiries that Chomsky and his associates are engaged in. I have no quarrel with the idea that in using language we display tacit knowledge, operating rules and principles that cannot in the normal way be brought to conscious formulation. Finally, I have no objection to innate mental structures on the grounds of their innateness. Obviously, human beings are born with certain abilities, including abilities to mature as well

[1] N. Chomsky, *Rules and Representations* (Columbia University Press/Blackwell, 1980), p. 39.

as abilities to learn. Whether the ability to acquire grammars of a certain kind is an ability to learn or an ability to mature under certain conditions seems to me a philosophically open question capable in principle of being settled by empirical inquiry.

Despite this range of agreement, I think that Chomsky employs in his writing a confused notion of the mental. I should perhaps begin by explaining what I think a non-confused notion of the mental looks like.

The mind is the capacity to acquire intellectual skills. The chief and most important intellectual skill is the mastery of language. Others, such as knowledge of mathematics, are acquired by human beings through the languages that they have mastered. So the study of the acquisition and exercise of language is the way *par excellence* to study the nature of the human mind.

Someone who has acquired a language *knows* that language. Knowledge of a language is an ability: an ability that can be exercised in many different ways, for instance, by speaking the language, by understanding what is said to one in the language, by reading the language, by talking to oneself in one's head in the language. To know a language just is to have the ability to do these and similar things. It is a conceptual truth that to study an ability you have to study the exercise of that ability: to investigate what the ability to φ is you have to investigate what φing is. So to study knowledge of language you have to consider and examine what the exercise of linguistic knowledge is. The exercise of linguistic knowledge can be called, if you like, linguistic behaviour. But 'behaviour' must be understood in a broad sense, so that, for instance, reciting a poem to myself in my head imperceptibly to others will count as an instance of my linguistic behaviour.

We must distinguish between abilities and their possessors on the one hand and their vehicles on the other. The possessor of an ability is what *has* the ability. I am the possessor of my linguistic ability; it is I (and not my mind, or my brain) who know English and am exercising this capacity in giving this lecture. Similarly, my car has the capacity to decelerate: it can go slower in answer to my touch on the foot-brake. The *vehicle* of the car's ability to decelerate is the brake mechanism; similarly, my eye is a part of the vehicle of my ability to see. The vehicle of an ability is that part of its possessor in virtue of which it is able to exercise the ability. A vehicle is something concrete and more or less tangible; an ability, on the other hand, has neither length nor breadth nor location. It is, if you like, an abstraction from behaviour.

An important instance of the distinction between possessor, ability, and vehicle is the distinction between people, their minds, and their brains. Human beings are living bodies of a certain kind, who have various abilities. The human mind is the capacity that human beings have to acquire intellectual abilities: a capacity is itself an ability, but a second-order ability, the ability to acquire abilities. The vehicle of the human mind is, very likely, the human brain. Human beings and their brains are physical objects; their minds are not, because they are capacities. This does not mean that they are spirits. A round peg's ability to fit into a round hole is not a physical object like the round peg itself, but no one will suggest it is a spirit. It is not any adherence to spiritualism, but simply concern for conceptual clarity, that makes us insist that a mind is not a physical object and does not have a length and breadth.

If a mind is not a physical object, can it have a structure at all? Yes, it can. The set of abilities through which the mental capacity is exercised have relationships to each other – there are relationships, for instance, between the ability to multiply and the ability to take square roots – and these relationships between abilities form the structure of the mind. Not only human beings have abilities that are structured in this way: we can discover the structure latent in the operations of a pocket calculator by identifying the algorithms that it uses. To discover the algorithm that a calculator uses, say, for the extraction of square roots calls for mathematical, rather than electronic, inquiry. When considering the human mind, the physiologist is in the position analogous to the electronic engineer, and the psychologist is in the position of a mathematician who is trying to deduce from the form the calculator's output takes (what kind of rounding errors it commits, etc.) what is the algorithm that it is using.

Chomsky makes a distinction between capacities and their vehicles, as I have done. He describes the objects of his study as 'human cognitive capacities and the mental structures that serve as the vehicles for the exercise of these capacities'. But in terms of the

distinctions that I have drawn the mental structures that Chomsky
is interested in are capacities, not the vehicles of capacities; it is the
physiological hardware characteristic of the exercise of the relevant
mental capacities that is the vehicle.

In fact Chomsky's mental structures seem to belong at times to
the world of software, at times to the world of hardware. The great
majority of what he says, as a linguist, about the knowledge and use
of grammar by language users, is perfectly intelligible in terms of
mental structures, being particular abilities and their exercises: the
exercise of the ability to operate an algorithm, to discover the value
of a particular grammatical function for a given grammatical
argument. But from time to time Chomsky the philosopher inter-
venes to tell us that what he is talking about is not to be understood
as a capacity or ability at all. It is something quite different, which
underlies the ability and its exercise, and which yet does not
underlie it in the way that the physiological structures and
processes of the brain do.

To show that it is possible to know a language without having
the capacity to use it, Chomsky offers the following argument:

> Imagine a person who knows English and suffers cerebral damage
> that does not affect the language centers at all but prevents their use
> in speech, comprehension, or let us suppose, even in thought.
> Suppose that the effects of the injury recede and with no further
> experience or exposure the person recovers the original capacity to
> use the language. In the intervening period, he had no capacity to
> speak or understand English, even in thought, though the mental
> (ultimately physical) structures that underlie that capacity were
> undamaged. Did the person know English during the intervening
> period? (p. 51)

The answer, Chomsky says, is 'yes': that is shown by the fact of
recovery.

I do not wish to contest the answer that Chomsky gives to his
question: what does seem to me surprising is his clear assumption
that there is a fact of the matter here, to be settled by considering
empirical evidence. If it really were a factual matter whether a
person in the condition described by Chomsky knew English or not,

then a thought experiment would be a most inappropriate way to settle the question. A thought experiment is not an experiment and does not provide empirical evidence: its function in philosophy is rather to draw attention to the shape and structure of our concepts. This Chomsky's illustration effectively does: it shows the fuzzy edges of the concept *knowing English*. In the normal case, a large number of criteria for the application of the concept are present: the person in question can readily speak, understand, and think in English. We imagine the criteria whittled away, so that all that is left is that the person is going later to use English normally. Shall we say he knows English in the interval? Well, we can say what we like as long as we know what we are doing: it is up to us to decide whether what is left is sufficient for us to call it 'knowledge of English'. Perhaps Chomsky is right that the more natural decision is to say that it is sufficient. Fine, then, let us say that the person knows English. But why should we not also say that the person retains the capacity to speak English? For extraneous reasons, he cannot use or exercise the capacity at the moment; but since, *ex hypothesi*, he is going to use it in future without any of the normal acquisition processes, is it not natural to say that he still holds on to it in the meantime? The concept of *capacity to use English* has exactly the same fuzzy edges as the concept of *knowledge of English* and Chomsky's example does nothing to separate the two concepts.

Of course, Chomsky denies the presence of the capacity during the intervening period. He says:

> In the intervening period, he had no capacity to speak or understand English, even in thought.

But why should he say that? It is possible that he thought that it followed from something else that is, on the hypothesis, genuinely true:

> He had no capacity to speak or understand English, even in thought, in the intervening period.

But, of course, the first proposition does not follow from the second, and if Chomsky thinks that it does he is mistaken.

Chomsky goes on to consider a second aphasic who is like the first but who never recovers speech. To deny that his person lacks knowledge of English would be perverse, he argues: we have agreed that the first aphasic knew English, and this second one is in exactly the same mental (ultimately physical) state, as might be shown on autopsy. Well, once again this would be a matter for decision, not for discovery; but surely this time the natural decision would go the other way. The one remaining prop to support the application of the concept *knowing English* – that the unfortunate was later going to use the language again without relearning – has been pulled away. So what grounds are left for saying that he knows English? 'But he is in the same brain state as somebody who does know English.' But that is to beg precisely the question at issue: that it is the brain state, and not the presence or absence of the capacity, that settles whether someone knows English or not.

The question-begging nature of Chomsky's procedure is masked by his use of expressions such as 'mental (ultimately physical) structures' and 'mental (ultimately physical) states'. Chomsky uses such expressions to indicate that his mentalism does not involve any sort of immaterialism: mental structures are simply physical structures described at a certain level of abstraction. But the expressions are ill-chosen, whatever one may think of immaterialism, because they conceal the fact that the criteria of identity for a mental state are not the same as those for a physical state. Two people can be in the same mental state while being in a different physical state, and can be in the same physical state while being in a different mental state. To say this does not beg any questions about materialism, since it is equally true of computers that there is no one – one correlation between software structures and hardware structures.

An analogy may help here. A monarch is a legal person, in the sense that what it is to be a monarch is defined by a set of legal relationships. But all actual monarchs, from Hammurabi to Elizabeth II, are physical persons, human beings of flesh and blood. We might therefore, in the style of Chomsky, call monarchs 'legal (ultimately physical) persons'. But if we do so, we invite confusion. Suppose that I met the King of England in 1937 and in 1940 I say, 'I have just met again the same legal (ultimately physical) person as I met in 1937'. Whom did I meet in 1940: the Duke of Windsor or King George VI? The confusion in talking of the same mental (ultimately physical) structure is less obvious but no less serious.

Indeed, the confusion is more serious. For monarchs are indeed persons; whereas states of the mind and states of the brain are not states of the same kind of thing. I agree with Chomsky that to describe a state of mind is to describe, at a certain degree of abstraction, a physical object; but the physical object so described is a human being and not a brain. The brain states characteristic of speakers of English – if we go along with Chomsky in assuming that there are such – may, for all we know, be reproducible in a brain *in vitro*. However successfully they were reproduced they would not constitute knowledge of English; for it is people, not brains, to whom it makes sense to attribute such knowledge.

Let me emphasize again that I am not arguing for immaterialism or spiritualism. The conceptual points that I have been making can be made about pocket calculators no less than about human beings. My calculator works out the square root of 123456789. In a flash, there comes the answer 11111.11106. Between my pressing the square-root key and the display appearing, complicated events took place in its electronic innards. Those events, whatever they were, could have taken place in a different calculator doing a different job; and a different calculator doing the same job might well have taken an electronically totally different route. Moreover, the hardware might have been taken out of the case, separated from the input keys and the output display. Whatever electronic events then took place inside it would not have been the working out of the square root of 123456789. For in the sense in which calculators can work out square roots for us, it is only whole calculators, and not portions of their electronic anatomy, however sophisticated, that can do the working out.

Chomsky's final argument against the identification of knowledge of English with the capacity to use it goes like this:

> Were we to identify capacity and knowledge, we would presumably be led to say that the aphasic does not know English when the capacity is lacking, and hence would be committed to the belief that

full knowledge of English can arise in a mind totally lacking this knowledge without any relevant experience whatsoever, as the case of recovery shows, something that is plainly not true of the child's mind and seems an exotic claim. (p. 52)

Such a claim would indeed be exotic; which makes it more surprising that only forty pages later, on p. 93, Chomsky should commend Arthur Danto for pointing out the possibility 'that in principle there might be a "Spanish pill" with the property that by taking it we should have been caused (adventitiously) to be masters of Spanish without having learned the language'. Such a master of Spanish would undoubtedly know Spanish, Chomsky says, hence

> We cannot rule out in principle the possibility that taking a pill might bring about the mental state that constitutes knowledge of Spanish.

In such a case, of course, knowledge of Spanish would arise in a mind totally lacking the knowledge without any relevant experience whatsoever: the claim that Chomsky dismissed as exotic in the earlier passage. Indeed it is a more exotic claim, for in the case of the recovered aphasic it might well be claimed that there *was* relevant experience: the experience at the time when the language was originally acquired in the normal way.

I think that Chomsky is right not to reject as inconceivable the notion that a pill might give us mastery of Spanish: the inconsistency between this concession and his earlier position merely brings out further the futility of his attempt to separate knowledge of English from the ability to use – the mastery of – the language. The idea is indeed exotic, but it is not literally inconceivable. What would be inconceivable would be the idea that a pill might give one knowledge of Spanish *without giving one the capacity to use the language.*

The root of Chomsky's confusion is his failure to distinguish between two different kinds of evidence that we may have for the obtaining of states of affairs: to distinguish between *criteria* and *symptoms* (to use the terminology introduced by Wittgenstein). Where the connection between a certain kind of evidence and the conclusion drawn from it is a matter of empirical discovery, through theory and induction, the evidence may be called a *symptom* of the state of affairs; where the relation between evidence and conclusion is not something discovered by empirical investigation, but is something that must be grasped by anyone who possesses the concept of the state of affairs in question, then the evidence is not a mere symptom, but is a *criterion* of the event in question. A red sky at night may be a symptom of good weather the following morning; but the absence of clouds, the shining of the sun, etc., tomorrow are not just symptoms but criteria for the good weather. Similarly, the occurrence of certain electrical brain patterns may be, or may some day come to be, symptoms of the presence of knowledge of English in the person whose brain is in question. But his ready use of English is not just a symptom of, it is a criterion of, a knowledge of English.

To grasp the importance of the distinction between criteria in symptoms in connection with knowledge of language, consider the following case. Suppose that Professor Chomsky were now to die, and on opening his skull we discovered that there was nothing inside it except sawdust. This is indeed an exotic suggestion: if it happened it would be an astonishing miracle. But if it happened it would not cast the slightest doubt on what we all now know, namely, that Chomsky knows English extremely well. But on Chomsky's view we would have to say that in fact it showed he never knew English at all, since on his view knowledge of English is ultimately a certain physical structure. But the supposition that someone can use English as Chomsky does and yet not know English is not just a miraculous supposition: it is a piece of literal nonsense.

Chomsky's characterization of the mental structures that interest him makes them straddle uneasily the distinction between hardware and software. They seem to be too ghostly to be hardware (from time to time he reminds us that it is no part of his theory that they should be in the brain rather than in the liver); but they also seem to be too concrete to be software, otherwise they could not be characterized as ultimately physical structures. But though his characterization of mental structures is, I have argued, confused and incoherent, what he is studying when he is studying mental structures is something genuine, important and fascinating. It is precisely the relationship between different capacities and sets of capacities.

Chomsky would deny this. If we reject his conception of mental structures, he says,

> We are left with a descriptive study of behavior, potential behavior, dispositions to behave and so on, a study that in my opinion cannot, in the end, be pursued in a coherent way . . . (p. 50)

What in fact we are left with, and what Chomsky in fact studies, are relations between different abilities: in particular the ability to render the value of certain functions (e.g. linguistic transformations) for given arguments. It is abilities of this kind that Chomsky is studying when he aims to uncover the structures underlying our use of language.

There are many intellectual tasks that we can perform in more than one way. When we multiply a number by ten, for instance, we can (a) simply add a 0 (b) recite the appropriate part of the ten times table (c) write the number down ten times and add up the result. Now, wherever we have a case of doing A by doing B there will be questions to be raised about the relations between the ability to do A and the ability to do B; we can only multiply by ten in the first way, for instance, if we know the decimal notation, and in the second way if we know the ten times table. And when we do A by doing B, it may well be that we know very well that we are doing A, but do not know without reflection that we are doing B; when we return a serve at tennis there are many movements of hand and arm that we are not normally aware of by which we make the return. Similarly, in performing intellectual tasks – including the comparatively modest ones of pronouncing a word or constructing a sentence – there are many sub-tasks that we perform without conscious advertence. When we ask what rules or principles we employ in performing these tasks, we are asking what sub-abilities we are exercising when we exercise the ability to use language.

In what sense, then, does the performance of such tasks have 'psychological reality' when it is not conscious? The ability being exercised is a *psychological* reality in the sense that it is an ability that is being exercised in a task that is an intellectual one and not a merely physical one. It is a psychological *reality* in that it is open to testing which of the various possible algorithms that I might use in performing the task is the one that I am actually using. It is here that it is relevant to study the reaction time of subjects and similar phenomena to which Chomsky's attitude has become increasingly cavalier.

I entirely agree with Chomsky in regarding the consciousness of a mental process as being quite inessential to the reality of the process. But this does not mean that psychological reality is unimportant. Once again, the point can be made in terms of simple non-human machines. It is a genuine empirical question which particular algorithm is being used by a computer or calculator to produce the solution to a problem, and the speed of computation and the nature of rounding errors and the like might provide empirical evidence for or against the use of a particular algorithm. It would in no way count against this that there was no representation of the algorithm in the output display of the calculator, or in the monitoring file provided by the computer. It is the monitoring file that is the analogue, in the computer context, of the conscious account that we can give of the way in which we perform intellectual tasks.

The philosophical confusions that I have claimed to detect in Chomsky's presentation of his theories of knowledge of grammar are in no way organic to the theories themselves. The theories, if I have understood them, can be stated in such a way as to be quite free of the particular form of mentalism in which they have been wrapped up and which has provided irrelevant distraction to philosophical and psychological critics.

Index